# EXPLORING

# WORLD ART

# EXPLORING

# WORLD ART

# Andrea Belloli

The J. Paul Getty Museum
Los Angeles

For my mother, in memory of Frances Godwin

At the J. Paul Getty Museum: Christopher Hudson, Publisher; Mark Greenberg, Managing Editor;
Shelly Kale, Editor; Kurt Hauser, Designer

First published in Great Britain in 1999 by Frances Lincoln Limited, 4 Torriano Mews, Torriano Avenue,

London NW5 2RZ

Belloli, Andrea  P.  A. Exploring world art/Andrea Belloli. p.   cm.
Includes index. Summary: Introduces the world of art, placing Western European art in a broad global context and discussing
artistic treatment of such themes as other worlds, daily life, history and myth, and nature.
ISBN 0-89236-510-2
1. Art --Themes, motives Juvenile literature.  2. Art appreciation Juvenile literature. [1. Art appreciation.] I. Title.
N7440.B35  1999
99-26521
CIP
709--dc21
Designed by Clair Watson

Set in Bembo
Printed and bound in KHL Printing Co Pte Ltd, Singapore
1 3 5 7 9 8 6 4 2

# Acknowledgments

Friends, acquaintances and complete strangers
made it possible for me to write this book. I'd like,
first of all, to thank my much-loved pal Patricia Williams.
Two writers who (unknowingly) inspired me were Erika
Langmuir and the fabulously wacky Maira Kalman.
I'd also like to acknowledge the consistent encouragement
and creative thinking (in every kind of weather) of Kate Cave
and "all the Cathys" at Frances Lincoln, most particularly my
alter ego Cathy Herbert, who hacked through my jungly prose
with precision and perceptiveness. My daughter, Sabina Aran, the
best advertisement I know of for exposure to art at a young age,
egged me on toward the finish line. Ian Powling, my partner, put
up with a lot of nonsense, kept me sane and pointed me in
the right direction throughout. Finally, Fred the Cat was on
hand most days to remind me of how important it is to eat
and stretch regularly and get plenty of sleep.

In addition to acknowledging the inevitably benign London
Library, I'd also like to thank the following individuals
and institutions for information and hospitality:

Margaret Birley at the Horniman Museum, London; Sue Beeby and Hans Rashbrook
at the Museum of Mankind, London; Aileen Dawson, R. B. Parkinson, David
Thompson, Rachel Ward, and Michael Willis at the British Museum, London;
Nicola Beech, Karen Brookfield, Michelle Brown, Julian Conway, and Frances Wood
at the British Library, London; Viviane Baeke at the Musée Royal de l'Afrique Centrale,
Tervuren; Professor Leopold Pospisil at the Peabody Museum of Natural History, New
Haven; Celia Oliver and Robyn Woodworth at the Shelburne Museum, Vermont;
Gordon Baldwin, Dawson Carr, Ken Hamma and Chris Hudson at the J. Paul Getty
Museum, Los Angeles; Jeremy Coote at the Pitt Rivers Museum, Oxford; John Villiers;
and Anabel Thomas.

# Contents

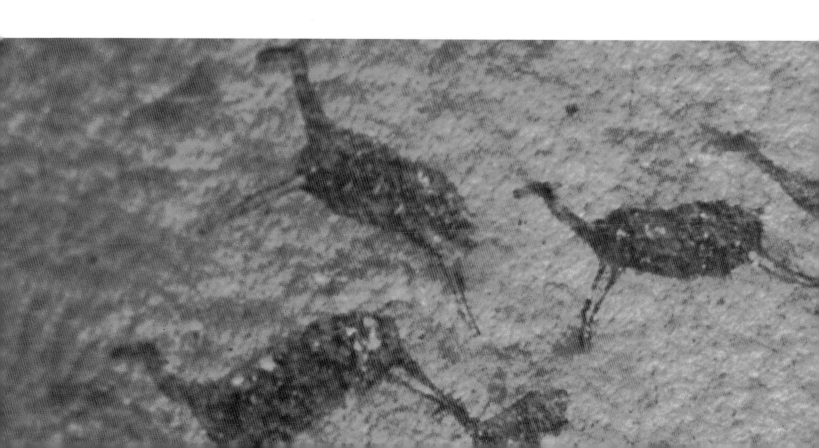

# Introduction

IMAGINE THAT YOU'RE A Native American elder celebrating the new year with your friends. You're trying to decide what the most important event was during the past year: the violent snowstorm that cut off your camp from the outside world for days, the battle in which many of your people were killed, or the spectacular meteor shower that dazzled all of you. How do you choose?

Now try imagining that you're a teenager in Central Africa, about to be acknowledged as a grown-up by your community in a special ceremony. You've been taken away from your family to prepare for the day; you and your friends have a lot to learn in a very short time. Are you excited or frightened? Maybe a bit of both. Will you be able to remember all of your new responsibilities?

Or imagine that you're an Armenian princess who's challenged a famous prince to a game of polo. Or a Persian scribe up to his ears in paperwork. Or a wealthy Frenchwoman getting ready for a fancy-dress ball. Or an ancient Egyptian frightened of dying.

You can find all of these characters in this book. The artists and artisans who created the objects and pictures illustrated here, and the people they created them for, had worries, hopes, fears, and plans just like you do. They were excited by special events, saddened by disasters, and amazed by things they'd never seen before. One way they tried to understand, represent, and come to terms with their worlds was by making art; like you, they were as interested in what went on inside their heads as they were in what went on around them.

Looking at these pictures and objects and trying to understand why they were created and what they might mean is like making a connection across time and space with their makers and users. It's a bit like time travel or visiting an unfamiliar planet: you may find yourself in unknown territory, trying to understand a foreign language, read strange writing, or become familiar with ideas and ways of behaving that make no sense at first.

But if you keep looking, you'll begin to see connections in the world of art and in your own life. You'll find people wearing masks while they dance in Paris and in Central Africa. You'll find that communication with the dead was as important in ancient China as it was in ancient Egypt. People saved expensive materials for recycling in both North America and Tibet, and depended on the repeating cycle of the seasons in Mexico and the Netherlands. We enjoy and worry and wonder in our time as people always have done. That's why art that was created many years ago, even by people with a completely different way of life from the one we know, still has the power to say something to us today.

Andrea Belloli

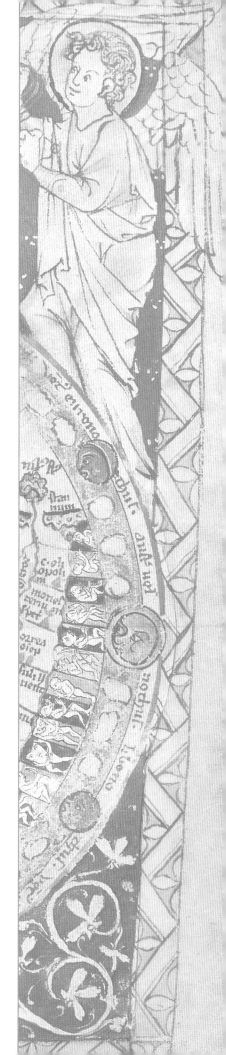

# Time and Space

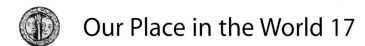

# Our Place in the World

IF YOU GET LOST, one way to figure out where you are is to look at a map.

Maps help us find our place in the world. They're based on millions of measurements collected by sailors, mountain climbers, explorers, and surveyors – nowadays even by satellites circling the globe.

Maps have changed a lot since the thirteenth century, when this one was made. In those days, crossing the oceans was unheard-of, and Europeans knew very little about lands beyond Europe, Africa, and Asia. Their maps were based on ancient myths and the Bible as well as on reports by travelers. Map makers were more interested in representing the world according to Christian belief than in creating an accurate diagram of the earth's surface.

This world map shows God, orb in hand, blessing the earth. The orb is a miniature model earth, a symbol of power. Angels swing incense burners as a sign of respect for God. A couple of two-legged dragons called wyverns lurk at the bottom of the map as a reminder that dangers lie in wait in unknown places.

According to this map, the center of the world and the center of the Christian faith are one and the same: Jerusalem, where Christ died and was resurrected. The wall at the upper left of the map surrounds the evil kingdom of Magog, whose inhabitants were expected to overrun the earth on Judgment Day. Along the right edge of the map are fourteen humanoid creatures that were thought to live in Africa. Above their heads, the River Nile flows toward its delta. Everything is based on Christian beliefs and comes under God's command.

### THE GARDEN OF EDEN

The face just below God on the map represents the East wind blowing down onto two other faces on either side of a tree. This is the Garden of Eden, and the faces are those of Eve and Adam, beside the Tree of Knowledge. Eden was thought to be the source of all the world's great rivers, so the Ganges, Tigris, Nile, and others flow out of a tunnel beneath it.

### PSALTER WORLD MAP
*England, early 1260s*

This tiny world map comes from a Psalter, a book of psalms. It shows Asia at the top, Europe at the bottom left, and Africa at the bottom right. The T-shape dividing the continents is the Mediterranean Sea.

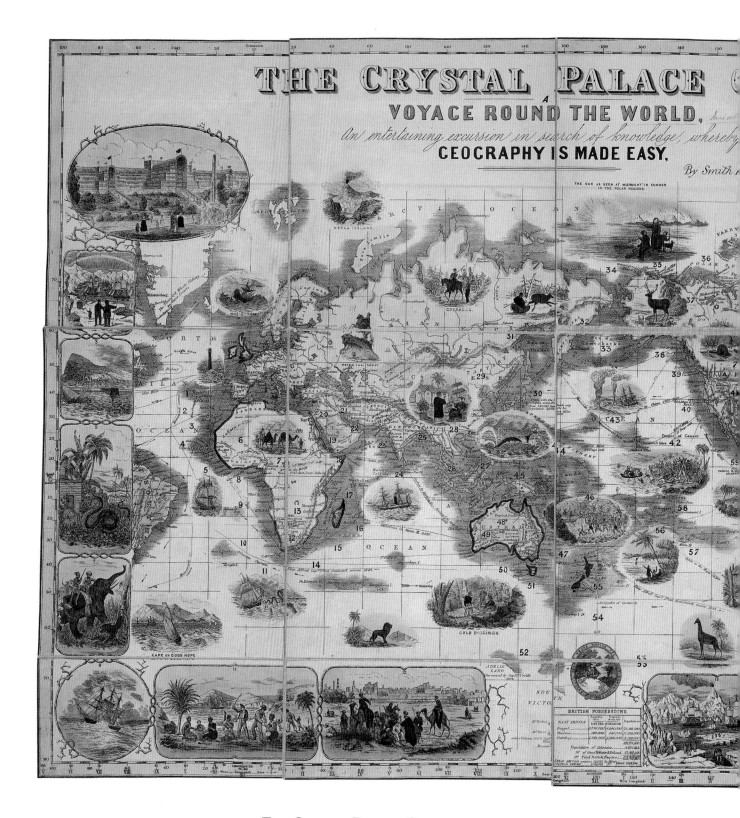

## THE CRYSTAL PALACE GAME

*Smith Evans, England, 1854*

This board game shows how Europeans' knowledge of the world had changed beyond
recognition since the creation of the Psalter world map six hundred years earlier.
The Crystal Palace itself is shown in the oval frame at the top left of the map.

In the centuries after the Psalter world map was made, long-distance travel became easier. Europeans began to map the earth in a more scientific way with the help of sophisticated instruments. After 1650, when it became possible to measure longitude – the distance east or west of an imaginary line running north/south around the globe through Greenwich, England – distances could be calculated more accurately. Unknown places were explored, and maps had to be redrawn. When it became clear that Magog and the scaly-tailed wyvern didn't exist, they disappeared from most maps.

But Europeans were still fascinated by people and creatures they considered exotic. In the nineteenth century, they organized huge international exhibitions to celebrate the world in all its complexity. One of the most famous shows was mounted in London in an enormous glass house called the Crystal Palace. The souvenir Crystal Palace Game helped children learn geography. The board shows distances and sailing times between ports – an indication of how ordinary it had become to travel from one end of the world to the other. The emphasis of the game, like that of the exhibitions, was on real life rather than fantasy. So it may come as a surprise to know that the man who designed it couldn't resist putting a monster just like a wyvern on his map! Can you find it?

### WONDERS OF THE WORLD

The board game illustrates a host of wonders: the midnight sun at the North Pole; violent storms at sea; huge whales with their water spouts; Canadian beavers building a dam. Here, two Indians riding a trumpeting elephant are startled by a tiger.

# What Do the Stars Foretell?

 DO YOU KNOW WHAT YOUR STAR SIGN IS? Do you ever look up your horoscope to see what the future holds?

If so, it's not surprising: people have been stargazing ever since ancient Babylon, when they first noticed groups of stars shaped like animals, birds, and people. Many hundreds of years later, the Greeks named these star groups signs of the zodiac, from the Greek word meaning "circle of animals."

By the thirteenth century, when this pen box was made, many people believed that the sign of the zodiac and the position of the planets when a person was born influenced his or her character, talents, and destiny. Star signs were also important when choosing a husband or wife, or a lucky time to do things.

Persian craftsmen such as Mahmud ibn Sunqur wanted to remind people of their beliefs as they went about their ordinary life. The craftsmen did this by

**PEN BOX**

*Mahmud ibn Sunqur*
*Persia, 1281-82*

This brasswork box was made to hold pens and ink in the days before printing, when scribes copied books and documents by hand. It is decorated with designs representing the signs of the zodiac and the planets. Inside the lid (looking from left to right), the crescent moon, Mercury, Venus, Mars, Jupiter, and Saturn are shown wearing long robes called kaftans, sitting cross-legged in a row on either side of the sun. The top of the box is decorated with three disks, each framing four signs of the zodiac.

decorating everyday objects with words or symbols. They sometimes used figures representing the planets, often with one of their associated signs of the zodiac, surrounded by arabesques – swirling patterns made up of plants, birds, and animals, like those on the sides of the box.

In Mahmud ibn Sunqur's day, most people could not read or write. Scribes – whose job it was to copy books and documents – were considered important because they could. The decoration on the pen box was meant to bring luck to its notable owner and remind him of his place in a complex yet orderly universe.

## How were the patterns made?

First the main designs were cut into the brass. Then tiny bits of contrasting metal – such as silver, gold, or copper – were hammered on as inlays. Further details – like facial features and the patterns on the clothes – were cut into the inlays themselves.

### A Disk on the Pen Box Lid

This disk on the top of the pen box lid shows Leo with the sun warming his back, Mars grasping two scorpions by their tails (Scorpio), the scales of Libra behind someone playing a stringed instrument called a lyre (representing Venus), and Virgo and Mercury working the land.

# Feeding the Sun

THIS AZTEC CALENDAR STONE tells a story about time since the world began.

The Aztecs ruled over the last great empire in the area we know today as Mexico. By the time they were conquered by Spanish colonizers in 1519, they had lived in the region for over two hundred years. They cultivated the land and built great cities with pyramids, palaces, canals, causeways, and temples – and they made complicated ritual sculptures such as the calendar stone.

The outermost border of the stone, made up of two fierce fire serpents, surrounds a calendar: a circle of pointed solar rays and a loop divided into sections containing signs for the twenty days of the Aztec month, one of which you can see in the detail on the left. At the end of each month there were ceremonies that included music, processions, and sometimes human sacrifices.

The carvings at the center of the calendar stone tell an even older story. One of the Aztecs' myths claimed that the earth had been created five times. Each time it lasted for a period known as a "sun," before ending in disaster. In cosmic time, the Aztecs were living in the fifth sun. The fearsome face at the center of the stone is this fifth sun itself. To the left and right of the sun's face are its claws, squeezing human hearts. The suns were thought to be gifts to the human race; human sacrifices were a way of paying back the debt by "feeding" them.

The Aztecs saw time as a system rather like the rings on the calendar stone: past and present spinning around in a series of never-ending circles. Human sacrifices recycled energy from human society to the natural world, helping to make sure that the system continued.

### THE AZTEC CALENDARS

The Aztecs used two calendars: a 365-day one for ordinary purposes, and a 260-day one for rituals. On the ritual calendar, days were shown by symbols called glyphs, and numbers by a system of dots and bars. Days were named after animals, birds, plants, and natural elements such as rain, but there were also days called House, Flint, and Death. This glyph from the calendar stone shows the day known as Lizard.

## HOW WERE THE CARVINGS MADE?

Like other Mesoamerican peoples, the Aztecs used tools made from obsidian, a glasslike volcanic stone, to carve decorative reliefs and sculptures. Obsidian is very hard and is sometimes even sharper than steel. It is still used to make surgical instruments.

## CALENDAR STONE
*Aztec, 1427*

This massive slab of basalt rock was found buried beneath a plaza in Mexico City in the late 1700s. The elaborate carvings are both a ritual calendar and a diagram of an Aztec creation myth.

# Time's Hidden Machinery

 THIS AMAZING SHIP-SHAPED CLOCK had a hidden message for an emperor's subjects.

Metal robots that measured time were very popular in Europe during the Renaissance. Hans Schlottheim, who made the clock, or *nef,* shown here, worked at the court of the Holy Roman Emperor Rudolf II as the official maker of automata, or models driven by hidden mechanisms. Among the other things he made were a musical model of the Tower of Babel and a life-size animated lobster of copper and brass.

Hidden inside the *nef* is an ingenious combination of steel gears, bellows, springs, and wheels. When the *nef* was wound up, it did far more than tell the time: the ship moved forward, bobbing up and down on its wheels as if riding the waves. As it moved, organ pipes played a fanfare, accompanied by hammers beating a drum, while on deck painted metal pipers and drummers moved back and forth in time with the music. Then the ship stopped while a circle of courtiers revolved around the figure of the emperor, who sat on a lion throne beneath a canopy. Once all the courtiers had passed in front of the emperor, the *nef* fired its cannon, and moved forward again.

What was the point of all this? We know that Emperor Rudolf II owned a *nef* made of silver. He may have ordered this less valuable one as a gift for a foreign ruler. In the age of exploration, ships were important: they were associated with trade, military strength, and prestige, and they reminded Europeans of their growing links with unexplored, mysterious lands.

The *nef* may have had a deeper meaning, too: philosophers of the time referred to God as the "divine clockmaker," and to princes as the "clocks of their countries." The clock face on the *nef* is right in front of the emperor's throne, below the crest of the Holy Roman Empire. Perhaps this was a way of telling people that the person who kept society ticking was the emperor himself.

**RUNNING LIKE CLOCKWORK**

Four hundred years ago, the Holy Roman Empire stretched over most of what we call Spain, Germany, Austria, and the Netherlands today. The Emperor was one of the most powerful rulers in the world. The double-headed eagle above the clock face is the Empire's crest.

**AUTOMATED SHIP OR NEF**
*Hans Schlottheim*
*Holy Roman Empire, about 1585*

This table clock is called a *nef* from an old French word for ship. It is made of copper, gilded to look like gold, and it was probably on show on special occasions such as banquets. The enamel clock face at the base of the tallest mast told the hours and minutes. Lookouts in the crows' nests struck bells with hammers to mark the quarter-hours.

# Stopping Time Dead

IN FAIRY TALES AND MYTHS, characters sometimes set out to make time stand still.

In the seventeenth century, people in the Netherlands were also very aware of how quickly life rushes by. Although the economy was booming and many people were doing well, they were wary of celebrating their good luck. The Bible warned them that riches are only temporary, and that all good things come to an end.

One way Dutch artists found to express this idea was through still life: paintings of everyday things like furniture, plants, and arrangements of fruit and vegetables. Some of these show elaborate vases of exotic flowers. At first sight the blooms seem perfect, but look again and you'll see tiny insects chewing the leaves. "Flower pieces" like these show nature's energy and beauty, but they also remind us that nothing lasts forever.

David Bailly's *Still Life* takes this idea a step further. The picture includes symbols of time passing or wasted – the hourglass, the smoker's clay pipe, the drunkard's wine glass – and of death – a skull and snuffed candle. The soap bubbles suggest the fragility of life. The young painter who looks out at us so seriously is holding a portrait of an older man whose face looks rather like his own. Bailly was sixty-seven when he painted *Still Life*. Does it show him as a young man imagining what he would look like as a mature, successful one? The objects strewn about the table are a reminder of the achievements of different kinds of artists: sculptors (the bust and statue on the right), metal-workers (the flower vase), jewelers (the pearls), musicians (one end of a recorder above the artist's right hand), and painters (the palette on the wall).

By placing himself in this lively setting, holding his own future in his hand, Bailly gave a hopeful twist to this otherwise somber picture: death is inevitable, but art can triumph over time by making its subjects immortal.

## WHAT IS AN ALLEGORY?

As well as being a picture of the untidy corner of an artist's studio, *Still Life* is an allegory – it contains a hidden meaning. The painting works on two levels: as a description of the things it shows you and as a message about what they mean.

**STILL LIFE**

*David Bailly, Netherlands, 1651*

Every item in this painting is realistically presented
and easily recognizable. Like many other Dutch
painters of his time, Bailly tried to paint objects so
that there could be no confusion about what they
were or how they related to each other.

# The First Moving Pictures

 BEFORE PHOTOGRAPHY WAS INVENTED in the middle of the nineteenth century, it was almost impossible for painters and sculptors to show people and animals moving as they do in real life. Our eyes simply don't have enough time to appreciate very quick, complicated movements and analyze them correctly. Because of this, painters and sculptors sometimes made mistakes and showed animals or people in impossible or unlikely positions.

This began to change when Eadweard Muybridge designed a special camera shutter that opened and closed just like a human eye but much more quickly.

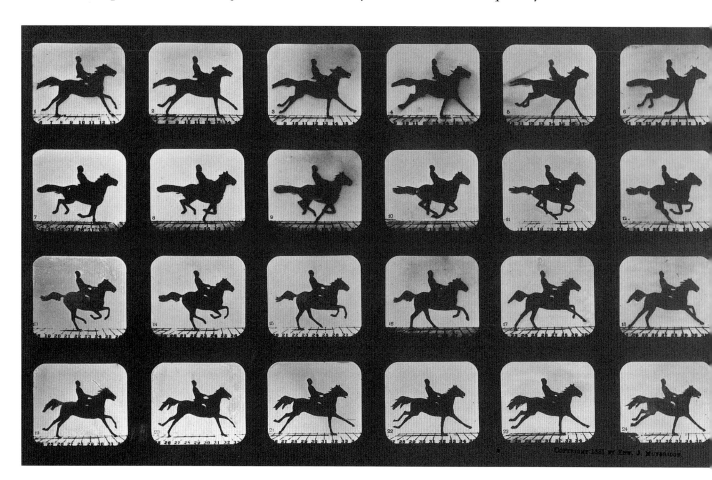

**GALLOPING**

*Eadweard Muybridge, England, 1878-79*

This series of photographs breaks down the continuous
movement of a galloping horse into a sequence
of separate moments, like snapshots. Muybridge sold
his pictures individually or in volumes called
*Animal Locomotion.*

## A FLYING HORSE

When a horse gallops, at one
point all four hooves are in the air,
tucked up under the horse's belly.
For a split second, the horse
almost seems to be flying!
No one was able to prove
this until Muybridge did his
photographic experiments.

With this camera, he was able to capture the details of
figures in motion, and publish series of photographs of
animals running and jumping, and of people walking,
leaping, climbing stairs, and doing sports and acrobatics.

In 1873 an American racehorse owner, Leland Stanford,
asked Muybridge to photograph his horse Occident, to help
him prove that when a horse gallops there is a moment
when all four hooves are off the ground at the same time.
Spurred on by this challenge, Muybridge perfected his
shutter and used a series of cameras to record how animals
and people really move through space.

When a magazine published some of the pictures, it
invited readers to cut them out and paste them around a
zoetrope – a small twirling drum mounted on a spindle.
As the zoetrope spun, the pictures appeared to flow into
one another, making it seem as if the figures really were
moving. Zoetropes and similar machines were the
ancestors of modern film-projection equipment – so you
could say that Muybridge's photographs helped pave
the way for the films we see today.

### HOW WERE
THE PHOTOGRAPHS TAKEN?

Muybridge set up a row
of cameras alongside
a race track. As the horse
galloped by, it broke
through a series of fine
wires attached to the
cameras' shutters, setting
them off one after the other.
In this way Muybridge
captured a lively sequence
of images of the horse in
motion on the light-sensitive
glass plates inside
his cameras.

# Painting the Dreamtime

 THE NATIVE PEOPLES OF AUSTRALIA – the Aboriginal Australians – give the name "Dreamtime" to the time when the world was created. They believe that during the Dreamtime, ancestral beings rose out of the earth and journeyed across the land, shaping it and laying down rules about how people should behave. When the Dreamtime ended, these beings disappeared or remained on earth in the form of features such as mountains, streams, and valleys. The Aboriginal Australians follow the ancestors' teachings. They believe that the land around these Dreamtime features belongs to them, and they create songs, dances, and short-lived paintings – in the sand, on rocks, or on their bodies – to preserve and celebrate the memory of the Dreamtime, when the landscape they live in was given its shape.

### YUPARLI JUKURRPA (BUSH BANANA DREAMING)

*"Butcher Jack" Japanangka*
*Australia, 1980s*

This Aboriginal Dreaming picture, painted with acrylic paints on canvas, may look like an abstract ocean of colored dots, but it has many meanings for Aboriginal viewers. It represents, on one level, the movements of ancestors through a Dreamtime landscape. It is also a map of the area that belongs to one Aboriginal clan. On a third level, it tells the story of two men who traveled from their own lands, returning finally to Pikily, a source of freshwater. The concentric circles may represent sacred Dreamtime sites or campsites, now sources of freshwater, and the wavy black lines a creeping plant called *yuparli*, which grows at each site.

In the past, Aboriginal Australians were hunter gatherers, moving from place to place according to the seasons. When English settlers arrived in Australia in the eighteenth century, they tried to make the Aborigines become Christians and live in towns. Like other native peoples, the Aborigines found it harder and harder to follow their traditional culture and way of life.

In the 1970s, however, Aboriginal artists realized that if they painted lasting versions of Dreaming pictures on bark or canvas, they could sell them and raise money for their people. These "dot paintings" show only what it is safe to let outsiders know. In this way, pictures like *Bush Banana Dreaming* help keep alive the memory of the Dreamtime, and with it traditional Aboriginal culture.

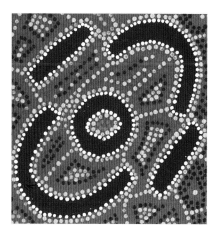

### UNDERSTANDING THE CODE

Dreaming paintings often have several meanings, and what you see in them depends on how much information you have. Here the U shapes represent people, and the bars beside them represent the sticks Aborigines use for digging up food.

### HOW WAS THIS PAINTING MADE?

Dreaming pictures were traditionally painted with red, yellow, white, and black paints made from plants and minerals. Many modern artists paint on bark or canvas with acrylic paints. Acrylics, used by "Butcher Jack" to make this lively painting, are made of synthetic rather than natural materials. They are popular because they are easy to work with, quick drying, long lasting, and produce bright colors.

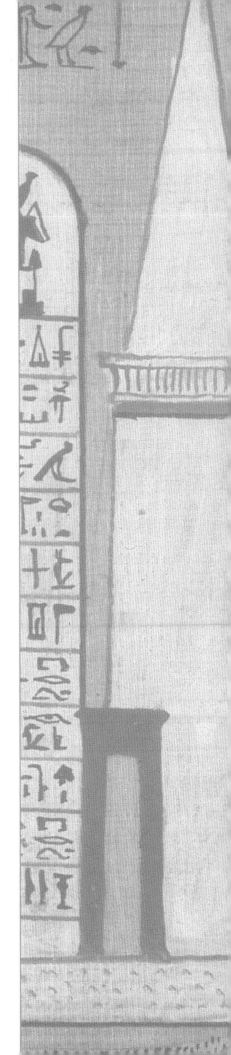

# Other Worlds

# Banquets for the Dead

PEOPLE IN MANY PARTS OF THE WORLD believe in some form of life after death.

In ancient China, people thought the dead were inhabitants of another world closely linked with this one. The dead could help the living and bring their descendants good fortune, so it was important to stay in touch with them. People made offerings of food and other good things to their dead ancestors on altars in homes and temples, laying out ritual banquets for the dead to share. Some of the offerings were made in bronze vessels and containers: tripods, basins, cups, cooking pots, wine flasks, and so on, each with a special name and use. The splendid ram-headed *zun* on this page and the *hu* on page 36 were both used for offerings of wine.

The oldest sets of decorated vessels discovered so far were made during the Shang dynasty, whose members founded one of the first Chinese states about four thousand years ago. Archaeologists exploring ruined Shang palaces, tombs, temples, and workshops have found objects made of jade, shell, pottery, metal, and bone. Among the discoveries were other offerings for the dead: weapons and equipment for the horses and chariots that were buried along with their royal or noble owners.

### BRONZE *ZUN*
*China, 17th-11th century B.C.*

This *zun*, used for offerings of wine, is a two-headed ram. The oval opening at the top grows out of the face of a monster with bulging eyes and two horns. The ram's back is locked in the monster's jaws.

**34**

The whole of this vessel is covered with hooked, scaly bands, which are meant to make you think of the spikes along a dragon's spine, but corrosion – the cause of the *zun's* turquoise-green coloring – makes some of the patterns hard to see. Like many other archaeological discoveries, this one had been in the ground for some time when it was found. When a metal object is buried for a long time, its surface can get pitted and scarred from chemical reactions between the metal and substances in the soil.

### REAL OR FANTASTIC?

In some ways the rams' heads on the *zun* are very realistic: horns, beards, soft-looking nostrils, and large eyes make them easy to identify. But the shape of the double-headed vessel, with its two sets of front feet, isn't at all like a ram's body. Shang artisans seem to have enjoyed mixing real and fantastic details to create lively, powerful images.

Some of the vessels in which offerings were made, like the *zun* on the previous pages, look like real or imaginary creatures, but the *hu* shown here looks more like a vase for flowers.

Whatever their shape, almost all the vessels are covered with complicated patterns. The meandering bands around the body of the *hu*, for instance, make up the head and body of a horned snake: two bulging eyeballs; a spiked nose with nostrils like a little anchor; and an open jaw with tiny teeth. The snake's horns are above its eyes.

Elaborate decorations like this are a clue that the owner of the vessel was someone rich and important, but the patterns had another meaning, too. In Shang China, snakes and dragonlike creatures were believed to have great strength and magical powers – perhaps because they were associated with the wind and the rain. When they used complicated snake or dragon patterns, the makers of the vessels were reminding people of these qualities. Perhaps they meant to give the vessels and their contents supernatural power that could be passed on to the spirits of the dead.

### A *TAOTIE* MASK

The symmetrical snake's head on the *hu* has a special name: a *taotie*. *Taoties* turn up on many objects that were made during the Shang period, although no one is sure what they represented.

### BRONZE *HU*

*China, 13th-12th century* B.C.

Each set of Shang bronzes included more than one vessel for wine, but we don't know why, or how, their uses differed. This *hu* looks like a simple vase with handles. The surface is decorated so that it appears to be covered with the skin of a horned snake. It's almost as if a real snake or lizard skin had been pounded flat and then wrapped carefully around the *hu*.

### HOW WERE SHANG BRONZES MADE?

These vessels were made by bronze-casters. The first step was to make an exact clay model of the vessel. The second was to build a set of ceramic molds around the model: all the surface decoration on the model and the final bronze appeared in reverse on the molds. The next step was to remove the model and pour hot liquid bronze – a molten mixture of copper and tin – into the mold. When the bronze had hardened, the vessel could be taken out of the mold, filed, and polished.

# Voyage to the Field of Reeds

 IS THERE A KEY TO ETERNAL LIFE? Thousands of years ago, the ancient Egyptians believed there was, and that they knew how to find it.

A garden paradise, called the Field of Reeds, lay waiting on the far side of death if the proper procedures were followed. Ancient Egyptians believed that people had several different spirits, which were released at the moment of death. These spirits could survive only as long as the dead person's body was preserved. In a hot, dry climate this was no problem: the bodies of ordinary people were buried in the desert sand, where they dried out slowly and were preserved naturally for centuries. However, people like the scribe Hunefer, shown in the scene below, got special treatment.

In this picture, Hunefer is at an important stage in his funeral. His body has been washed and purified, and his internal organs removed. Oils and resins have been applied to his body to preserve it, and it has been tightly wrapped in strips of cloth and bandaged

to keep its shape, turning it into a mummy. A mask has
been placed on Hunefer's head. Now the priests standing
to the left of the women mourners are ready to perform
the Opening-of-the-Mouth ceremony. Two of them
are about to touch Hunefer's face with a chisel, an adze,
and a snake stick to restore his soul and senses so he can
use them in the afterlife. (The chisel and adze are sculptors'
tools; this ceremony was originally performed to bring
statues to life.)

When all the ceremonies and procedures were complete,
the mummy was put into a body-shaped coffin – or,
in the case of someone very important, a nest of coffins –
decorated with carvings and paintings of symbols and
scenes from the afterlife, and writings that were supposed
to give the dead person protection. Finally, the coffin was
taken to the tomb from which the dead person would set
out on the voyage to the Field of Reeds.

Ancient Egyptian tombs were cut into solid rock and
chapels were built above them at ground level. Hunefer's
is topped by a miniature pyramid. Tombs had several
chambers, and their walls and ceilings were covered with
paintings not just of the voyage to the Field of Reeds but
of daily life as well. Solid reminders of this world went
into the tombs, too, in the form of food, tools, clothes,
jewels, furniture, and small models of houses and people.

**OFFERINGS FOR THE DEAD**
Smoke rises from the incense burner
held by the priest who wears
a leopard skin and also carries a
small pitcher. Offerings for Hunefer,
including round loaves of unleavened
bread, are piled on the mat
in front of the priest.

**VIGNETTE SHOWING THE
OPENING-OF-THE-MOUTH CEREMONY**
*Egypt, 19th Dynasty, about 1310 B.C.*

This painting from the *Book of the Dead* shows
the mummy of a scribe called Hunefer, held
by a priest in a jackal mask representing the god
Anubis, who presided over everything to do
with funerals and mummification. An inscribed
gravestone stands behind the god. The pyramid
at the far right is Hunefer's burial chamber. Wealthy
people would commission personal selections from
the *Book of the Dead* to be buried with them.

WAS THE *BOOK OF THE DEAD* A BOOK?

The ancient Egyptians made paper
by pressing the pithy stems of papyrus plants
together. Instead of binding the sheets
up into books with pages, they kept them as rolls.
Hunefer's "book" contains spells and pictures
intended to help him avoid danger on his journey
through the underworld to the Field of Reeds.

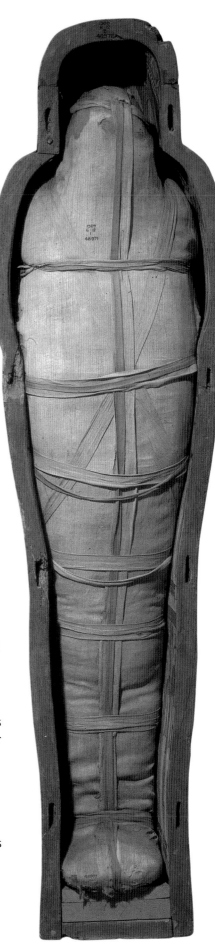

## WOODEN COFFIN AND MUMMY OF AN UNKNOWN PRIESTESS

*Egypt, 21st Dynasty, about 1000 B.C.*

The dead body of this priestess from Thebes, a religious center in Upper Egypt, was carefully wrapped in strips of linen and laid in a wooden coffin. The coffin follows the shape of the mummy and is decorated with elaborate painted symbols and scenes of life after death.

The paintings and sculptures found in the tombs of ancient Egypt show us what life was like at the time. The ancient Egyptians lived in the Nile valley, and they depended on the river's regular floods to make the land fertile. The tomb decorations show them fishing among the papyrus marshes, planting and harvesting food crops, and hunting birds and animals with boomerangs and bows and arrows. Texts written in hieroglyphics – a writing system that uses pictures to represent sounds – are also found in these tombs.

Another notable Egyptian whose body has been preserved for thousands of years is the priestess whose wooden coffin and mummy are shown on page 40. The wings painted on the lower half of the coffin were meant to place her under the protection of Isis, one of the goddesses worshipped in ancient Egypt.

Although we know nothing about this priestess, not even her name, the fact that her body was preserved and protected so carefully tells us that she was important enough to deserve special treatment as she set out for the Field of Reeds.

### PRIESTESS HENUTMEHIT'S PAINTED WOODEN SHABTIS AND *SHABTI* BOX

*Egypt, 19th Dynasty,
about 1290 B.C.*

When they died, Egyptians hoped to go to the Field of Reeds, a garden paradise. Wealthy Egyptians like the Priestess Henutmehit had sets of *shabti*s – small human figures shaped like mummies and often equipped with tools, seed bags, water pots, and baskets – put in their tombs to toil in the Field of Reeds so that they wouldn't have to do any work themselves. Sets of *shabti*s were placed in decorated chests like this one. If you look on the side of the chest, you can see the priestess worshipping three gods.

### THE ANNUNCIATION

*Dieric Bouts, Netherlands, about 1450-55*

This picture, which appears to be complete in itself, is actually
one of several panels from an altarpiece. Altarpieces were
rather like three-dimensional picture books, made of painted,
wooden parts joined together by hinges.

# A Heavenly Messenger

THE BIBLE IS FULL OF DRAMATIC MOMENTS when human beings meet supernatural ones.

One of these astonishing episodes is the Annunciation – the moment when the archangel Gabriel is sent from heaven to tell a young woman that she is to have a baby called Jesus, who will be the son of God. Gabriel is a kind of supernatural go-between, linking two worlds by carrying God's message down from heaven to the house in Nazareth (a town in present-day Israel) where Mary lives.

The Flemish painter Dieric Bouts chose to set his *Annunciation* in a sober medieval building, although he was painting something that had happened more than a thousand years earlier in another part of the world. The chilly stone walls make a strong contrast with the warm scarlet of Mary's bedclothes, reminding us of how hard it must have been to keep warm in homes like this.

Bouts treated the archangel's arrival with simplicity and respect. He arranged the scene the same way as many artists had done before him, so church-goers could tell easily what was going on. Bouts imagined Mary sitting on the floor of her room, deep in prayer, until Gabriel's arrival – perhaps through the window in the background – took her by surprise. The tips of Gabriel's wings, just outside the colonnade, almost seem to tremble – the only sign of the drama and excitement of the moment.

The body language of the two figures tells the story without words. Gabriel kneels, showing respect for Christ's mother; the message is conveyed simply by the angel pointing one pale finger. Mary looks modestly down at her lap, but her hands are raised as if to capture or give shape to the astonishing news the messenger has brought. Her posture suggests two ways of bridging the gap between the human and heavenly worlds to Christian viewers: prayer and unquestioning faith.

## HOW WAS THIS PAINTING MADE?

Bouts painted with distemper, a water-based paint held together with animal glue. He worked on pieces of linen, building up the picture surface with small brush strokes and fine layers of color; these are known as washes. This technique gave the painting its gently glowing surface.

## WHAT SEX IS AN ANGEL?

During the Middle Ages, people argued about whether angels were male or female – it was hard to decide if you had never seen one. Many artists painted angels as handsome young men, sometimes gently smiling and sometimes extremely serious, but Bouts's archangel – with plush wings, flowing hair, and loose robes – is more like a respectful humanoid.

# A Call to Prayer

 LIKE CHRISTIAN NUNS AND MONKS in medieval Europe, Buddhist monks in Tibet rely on music to signal when they should turn their thoughts to prayer. Conch trumpets like the one shown on page 45 are used to call monastic communities together five times a day to pray.

Buddhism reached Tibet from India across some of the world's highest mountains in the seventh century A.D., and became the national religion. The founder of Buddhism, the Indian nobleman Siddhartha Gautama, preached compassion for all living creatures.

A conch is a natural trumpet, and blowing one will produce a sound even without adding a mouthpiece, as was done here. Another addition is the twisting metal tube ending in a piece shaped like a lotus blossom (like the conch itself, the lotus is a symbol of good luck). Some conch trumpets have colorful fabric streamers suspended from the tube end. Others, like this one, have elaborate metal extensions of the shell's own "wing," often decorated with reliefs – raised patterns – showing clouds, sea monsters, and Buddhist symbols. These extensions direct and amplify the trumpet's sound.

Buddhist monks normally play conch trumpets in pairs, standing side by side. They are quite easy to play compared with other Tibetan wind instruments, so young monks are often given the task of blowing them. Conch trumpet music is supposed to have special qualities that make it highly appropriate within a monastery: like the sound of a bell or drum, it is said to drive away evil spirits, and – according to one Tibetan master – to carry the message of Buddhism to awaken monks from the sleep of ignorance. Because conch shells are found in the water, Tibetans also believe these trumpets have magical power over rain, so sometimes monks stand on temple roofs and blow them to ward off hailstorms.

### A LUCKY MONSTER

This monster flying through swirls of clouds over jagged peaks may look fierce, but the clusters of turquoise and other semiprecious stones surrounding it are a sign that it may bring good fortune.

## WHERE DID THE MATERIALS COME FROM?

Tibetans relied on trade for some
of the materials used to make this trumpet.
The conch shells themselves were carried
the huge distance from the sea along
hazardous routes across high mountains.
Pearls and other precious stones came
with traders from China.

## CONCH-SHELL TRUMPET
*Tibet, about 1800*

Made from a white conch shell, bronze, and jewels,
this trumpet was used to call Buddhist monks
to prayer. It has a metal mouthpiece and a long
tubular "tail." The metal "wing" with its tasseled
corner looks as if it's made of fabric, and so you
might expect it to hang down when the instrument
is played. In fact, it stands up, as shown below.

# A Man Becomes a God

## THE FACE OF A'A

All of A'a's facial features are made out of small carved figures that represent his descendants. The sculptor made the figures into eyes, ears, brows, cheeks, and mouth by adjusting their poses and rotating or clustering them.

IN POLYNESIA, a huge area of islands in the Pacific Ocean, islanders believed chiefs inherited their power directly from the gods. When chiefs died, they became gods themselves.

History – passed on by word of mouth from generation to generation – and family relationships were enormously important to the islanders. To be a chief, with a family tree that went right back to the gods or the mythological past, made you a very special person with many worldly and spiritual responsibilities.

Chiefs saw that traditions were passed on to future generations and regulated community life. This was not an easy job: life on the Polynesian islands could be harsh. Few food plants grew there, and islanders had to depend on fishing and on a few crops they planted themselves, such as yams, breadfruit, bananas, sugar cane, coconuts, and chestnuts. Chiefs were responsible for distributing food and coping with emergencies. Their prestige grew if they were good at doing this. In addition to food crops, the islanders planted trees and used the wood to build houses and make canoes, utensils, weapons, and statues.

Europeans first came to Polynesia in the eighteenth century. Very few wooden sculptures survive from before then, and in most cases we can only guess at what they meant or what they were used for. Luckily the British missionary who sent the figure of A'a back to England sent an explanation with it. We know from this that the large hole in the statue's back once contained a number of smaller images. These have been lost, but A'a himself is still covered with other small figures, some of which look a lot like him.

A'a was the ancestor of the ruling clan of Rurutu in the Tubuai Islands. The small figures represent his descendants. If these small figures weren't there, his body would lose its structure and its features – in fact, it would hardly be a body at all. In much the same way, Polynesians regarded the life of any one individual as meaningless apart from the lives of other members of the clan.

## THE GOD A'A

*Tubuai Islands, pre-1821*

This figure, nearly three and a half feet tall, represents the real-life chief of a clan on one of the islands in French Polynesia, who became a god after he died. The statue is made from a very hard wood called ironwood, and it has a large cavity in its back. In the early 1800s, when the figure was probably made, the islanders had no metal, so they would have used tools made of stone, shell, or animals' teeth to carve sculptures.

### HOW DID THE SCULPTURE GET TO LONDON?

Like many other objects from faraway places that are preserved in British museums today, the statue of A'a was collected by European missionaries and sent back to England to show how successful they had been at converting native peoples to Christianity. Similar objects from the Pacific and elsewhere made their way into museums through warfare, trade, purchase, scientific research – even outright theft.
Recently, some native communities have asked to have objects returned to them as a way of reclaiming their heritage.

# Spirits of the Hunt

HOW DO YOU SURVIVE when it's so cold that the sea turns to ice? For the Bering Strait Inuits, who live near the Arctic Circle, the key to survival lay in hunting, fishing, and acting out rituals to keep a balance between living creatures and the spirits who controlled their supply of food.

The Inuits believed that animals, birds, and even lifeless objects had souls. Fish, seals, caribou, and other creatures would allow hunters who treated them with respect to kill and eat them. The souls of the dead animals would come back to life. As long as the Inuits respected other living creatures and performed the traditional rituals, there would be plenty to hunt in the future.

In addition to being expert hunters, the Inuits were skilled at many crafts. When they caught an animal or bird, they kept its sinews, fur, or feathers to decorate wooden masks, like the one on page 49, which were used in ritual dances thanking the spirits for their generosity. To make these communications effective, the masks were carved to look like inhabitants of the spirit world. Since mask carvers were ordinary people who couldn't see spirits, they needed the help of a special person called a shaman who could visit the spirit world in dreams and trances.

Shamans reached the spirit world through a smoke hole in a dwelling or a hole in the ice. Once there, they asked the spirits, and the souls of dead animals, to look kindly on their communities. When they returned from their dream journeys, they told the mask carvers what they had seen. The carvers translated their descriptions into lively – sometimes frightening or humorous – sculptures.

Many of the masks express the Inuit idea of transformation: that it is possible to cross from one world to another, or view another world through an imaginary eye or hole. The Inuits' cycle of winter ceremonies invited spirits into the human world and then sent them back again, to maintain the balance of nature for another year.

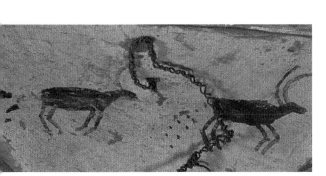

## CARIBOU ON THE RUN

The animals running across the doors of the mask are large deer called caribou. They roam the Alaskan tundra in constant search of food. They were especially prized by Inuit hunters because clothes made from caribou skin give very good protection against the cold.

## HOW WAS THE MASK MADE?

The Arctic is so cold that very few trees can grow there. The Inuits made their wooden masks from driftwood. They used iron tools for carving and painted the masks with dyes made from iron ore, clay, and ashes.

## TRANSFORMATION MASK
*Alaska, collected about 1880*

When the doors of this mask are closed, the wild-haired figure looks almost human. Open them and he is transformed into a thumbless, jagged-toothed *tunghak,* a spirit with power over animals. This spirit, which the Inuits said lived in the moon, helped shamans. Masks like this were used in winter ritual dances.

49

**NKONDI STATUE**

*Democratic Republic of the Congo,*
*about 1900*

This threatening carved wooden figure, spiked with a forest of nails and other bits of metal, represents a force from the world of spirits. Each metal spike corresponds to a request made to the figure to punish a wrongdoer.

# Mirrors and Medicine Packs

WHEN THINGS GO WRONG, we would all like a powerful friend to turn to. This wooden figure, bristling with nails and spikes, is one of the most powerful allies of all: an *nkisi*, used by the Kongo people of Central Africa to summon up help from the world of the dead.

The force these figures represent can help anyone who has been harmed or injured: the sick, victims of robbery or witchcraft, and so on. A violent *nkisi* seeks out and punishes wrongdoers, but there are kinder ones, too, that can intervene to bring people wealth and good luck. Both kinds of *nkisi* carry packs of substances known as "medicine" to reinforce their power. Clay and earth – symbols of death – make the *nkisi* more powerful by strengthening its link to the world of the dead. Other medicines may include anything that suggests the effects desired by the people who appeal to the *nkisi*.

This threatening figure is a special kind of *nkisi* – an *nkondi* - which was supposed to be of special help to chiefs. It bristles with spikes of all kinds: screws, nails, blades, and other bits of metal driven randomly into its head and body to activate its anger. The sheer number of spikes suggests that this was a very powerful *nkondi*, with a great reputation for skill and strength. Once it must have looked even more fearsome than it does now: its upraised arm held a spear or dagger, which would have pointed menacingly at anyone who dared stand before it. It would also have "worn" medicine packs on its head, back, and belly, each pack with a mirror (so people could make sure that there was no witch creeping up on them from behind).

A person who had been wronged could release the figure's power by sticking a spike into it and telling it how to act. Being "nailed" activated the *nkisi*'s anger, channeling energy from the world of the dead into the world of the living to help victims of injustice, illness, and misfortune.

## THE FACE OF A SPIRIT

The face of the *nkondi* is painted ghostly white to show that it is a spirit from the land of the dead. It stares straight ahead out of large glass eyes with dark pupils. Its mouth is wide open: people often asked figures like this to "eat" the wrongdoers who had injured them.

## WHERE DID THE NAILS COME FROM?

Most of the hardware sticking into the statue was made locally, but there are European screws and nails, too. The small bundles, pieces of string, and other tokens hanging from the statue were meant to point the *nkondi* in the right direction to do its work.

# Daily Life

# Preparing for Battle

 NOWADAYS IT'S EASY to find out what's been happening in the world. We can read a newspaper, log on to the Internet, or turn on the radio or television.

There were ways of letting people know about important events long before these inventions existed. It was common practice for rulers to hire artists to make pictures, prints, or carvings as souvenirs of important official occasions. These were put on display in public places to remind people of their history.

This example of public art from the ancient Americas shows the mighty Mayan ruler Lord Shield Jaguar with one of his wives. Shield Jaguar had to go through a series of demanding rituals when it was time for him to become king. He appeared before his people wearing a special costume. He and one of his wives then drew blood from their own bodies to nourish the Mayan gods. This bloodletting transformed Shield Jaguar into a supreme religious leader. After the bloodletting, Shield Jaguar went off to war: he had to bring back captives to prove that he was ready to be king.

This relief – a raised design on a flat stone surface – shows Shield Jaguar and his wife as he prepares for battle. The bands of picture symbols above them tell us the date in the Mayan calendar (the equivalent of February 12, 724 A.D.). Shield Jaguar wears armor over a long waistcoat, a headdress with floral medallions, cuffs around his wrists, and kneebands. His wife cradles his jaguar headdress in her arms.

## THE SACRED JAGUAR

Some of the Mayan gods took the forms of creatures of the tropical rainforest. One of these was the jaguar. Many Mayan lords had jaguar titles, and jaguar skins were associated with royalty.

## STONE LINTEL
*Maya, about 725 A.D.*

This battered limestone relief, carved over a doorway in a ceremonial building in the riverside city of Yaxchilan in Mexico, was once brightly colored (traces of paint can still be seen). It illustrates a solemn moment in the ritual when the Mayan ruler Shield Jaguar claimed his throne.

# Everyday Details

GETTING MARRIED is usually a time of joy and celebration, but it can also be a moment when people think carefully about their future.

Perhaps that's why the couple in *The Arnolfini Marriage* look so serious. The painting documents the marriage commitment in a symbolic way. The man – a successful Italian merchant, Giovanni Arnolfini – is shown as if he has just entered the room. He has taken off his wooden clogs to avoid bringing mud indoors, and has offered his hand to the woman who has been waiting for him. She has placed one of her hands in his, palm up, as if to show that she trusts him completely. She glances toward him shyly, perhaps overwhelmed by his presence.

Like other artists of his time, van Eyck paid attention to the little details that make a painted world convincing. These are just the kinds of furnishings a wealthy merchant might have owned: a large bed, a glistening chandelier, a fine wooden bench, and an expensive convex mirror. Light streams in through the window, revealing other telling details. The oranges on the sideboard and windowsill are exotic fruits from southern Europe, which would have been hard to come by in Flanders. The couple's clothes are trimmed with fur and made from many yards of expensive fabric.

The little dog may symbolize mutual faithfulness as well as obedience, a quality that Christian women in medieval and Renaissance Europe were expected to show their husbands. Other paintings of the time tell us more about women's lives during this period.

## WHO ELSE WAS IN THE ROOM?

Imagine that you are standing just outside the room van Eyck painted. What is between you and the dog? We can see two figures reflected in the mirror on the far wall. They could be witnesses to Arnolfini's marriage, ready to be presented to his new wife; one of them may even be the artist himself. However, the inscription on the wall above the mirror, "Only Jan van Eyck was here," suggests that the room may only have existed in the artist's imagination.

## THE ARNOLFINI MARRIAGE
*Jan van Eyck, Netherlands, 1434*

Two solemn-looking people pose for a double portrait with their dog in a narrow bedroom crowded with rich furnishings. They were probably Giovanni Arnolfini, an Italian merchant living in Bruges, and his second wife, whose name we do not know.

The *Magdalen Reading* was painted by the Flemish artist Rogier van der Weyden soon after van Eyck completed *The Arnolfini Marriage*, and it has a similar well-to-do setting. Its subject, Mary Magdalen, is seated on a large cushion on the wooden floor, leaning back against a sideboard with a carefully painted sliding bolt and delicate hinges. She wears a green robe, tightly pulled in with a sash. Her stiff brocade underskirt has a jeweled hem (maybe to remind people that she is an important figure from the Bible), but otherwise her robe and headcloth are more modest than those of van Eyck's female sitter.

The covers of Mary Magdalen's neatly bound Bible, prayer book, or Book of Hours, are protected by a piece of snow-white cloth, so the book must have been an object of value. If the artist's model could actually read, she may have come from the privileged circle around van der Weyden himself: women who could read were a rarity in fifteenth-century northern Europe, just as they were in biblical times.

## THE WORLD OUTSIDE

Van der Weyden and van Eyck both give us tantalizing glimpses of the wide world beyond the intimate spaces they painted. In van Eyck's *The Arnolfini Marriage* (on page 56) you can just see a cherry tree, heavy with fruit and blossom, outside the window. Similarly, van der Weyden has painted a view of a river, alive with tiny figures and leafy reflections, behind Mary Magdalen.

## HOW WERE THESE PAINTINGS MADE?

The artist van Eyck became famous in his lifetime for his mastery of the medium of oil painting. Oil paints form a solid film quite slowly, so van Eyck was able to spend time working (with brushes and fingers) on the tiny details that make his pictures so convincing. He also built up transparent paint layers called glazes to create glistening surfaces and deep shadows. Van der Weyden worked in oils, too; the ones he used in *The Magdalen Reading* were pressed from the seeds of the flax plant.

## THE MAGDALEN READING
*Rogier van der Weyden*
*Netherlands, about 1435*

According to the Bible, Mary Magdalen was possessed by demons until they were exorcised by Jesus Christ. After Christ was crucified, she went to his tomb to help prepare his body for burial. In the painting, the alabaster jar of ointment she took with her to the tomb sits on the floor beside her. You can see by the cutoff figures behind and to the left of Mary Magdalen that this is a fragment of a larger painting. The other figures are saints.

# Changing with the Seasons

 FOUR HUNDRED YEARS AGO, when most people in Europe still worked on the land, the seasons determined how they spent their time. This vivid miniature of May is from a page of a medieval Book of Hours – a selection of Christian prayers and meditations, which often included a record of regular events in the Christian year such as holidays, fairs, and festivals.

The twelve calendar pictures of the "Golf Book" – so called because it contains the earliest painting of people playing a game like golf – are packed with information about what people wore, where they lived, and how they passed their time over four hundred years ago.

**MAY FROM THE "GOLF BOOK"**
*Perhaps by Simon Bening*
*Netherlands, about 1530*

This miniature painting shows some of the ways wealthy people passed the time in May. Readers would have been able to identify the month from clues like the man playing the flute and the leafy branches around the boat: May was associated with music-making and with the green leaves of spring.

The small figures painted to look like carvings in the panel below the main picture may be children. Here they are practicing archery, but similar panels for other months show different seasonal activities, such as sledding, rolling hoops, or chasing butterflies.

Each miniature is set in a "frame" which is painted to look like carved wood. The pictures have the feel of scenes glimpsed through a window. Month by month they show peasants feeding their animals, baking bread, planting and harvesting crops, cutting down trees. In October they press grapes to make wine; in December they kill pigs for the Christmas feasting. For wealthy people, the year passed very differently: they are shown riding, hunting with dogs and hawks, taking part in jousts. In summer the miniatures show them relaxing in beautiful gardens; in winter enjoying food and drink.

At the time these scenes were painted, nobles and peasants led very different lives, but the pictures show us one important thing they had in common: daily life for everyone – rich or poor, at work or play, child or adult – changed with the changing seasons.

### JANUARY FROM THE "GOLF BOOK"

The bare branches here look bleak compared with the green leaves of May. Everyone is hard at work trying to keep warm. The peasants outside are splitting and gathering logs. The artist left one wall off the house so that we can look inside and see a couple with a baby huddled by the fire. The ice in the bowls on the bench shows just how cold it is.

### WHAT IS A MINIATURE?

A miniature is a painted picture in a manuscript, or handwritten book. When it is used like this, the word "miniature" has nothing to do with size: it comes from the Latin word *minium,* which means red, because early books had red decorations. Miniatures are sometimes called illuminations because they were usually made with colors that caught the light. Precious metals like gold and silver were also used, either as inks or as "leaves" — very thin sheets stuck to the page with gum or another adhesive.

# Party Time in Paris

FOR MORE THAN TWO HUNDRED YEARS, followers of fashion have watched the Paris designers to find out what the next season's "look" will be.

Paris became a trend-setting center in the eighteenth century. Painters like Jean-François de Troy were commissioned by powerful clients to produce pictures of aristocrats wearing the latest hairstyles and fashions. These pictures were often set in private spaces – women's bedrooms and sitting rooms – and the atmosphere was always lighthearted. The people in the paintings are getting ready to go somewhere, or on their way there, or returning home again – they're either looking forward to things or remembering them.

Here, a woman is getting ready to go out for the evening, surrounded by servants and friends. This is French high society, and de Troy invites us into the picture as if we belong there. The central figure is dressed in a brocade gown protected by one of the flowing robes popular at the time. Her lively gestures as she twists around in her chair look natural and unrehearsed. The man in blue leaning over the back of her chair holds a black mask with red tassels. Two people in the background are whispering together like conspirators. We can almost feel the excitement in the air!

Pictures like this may not show famous people or happenings, but they give a very lively impression of Parisian life in the 1700s.

**BY CANDLELIGHT**

Candlelight makes the surfaces look lively and warm while leaving the surroundings in deep shadow. The brightest light is reflected from the main figure's white robe and the excited faces form an almost perfect oval. De Troy was known as a generous host. By leaving part of the oval open, he invites us to join the group of gossiping friends.

**BEFORE THE BALL**
*Jean-François de Troy, France, 1735*

Despite its deep shadows and dark colors, this painting captures a moment of great anticipation. A maid arranges an elegant woman's hair as she chats excitedly with her friends, who are about to whisk her off to a masked ball.

# Fit for a Chief

IMAGINE THAT EVERY SINGLE PERSON IN AMERICA had a whisk to fan flies away during long, hot summers. Now imagine that the President had one – his would be special because of who he is. Like this chief's fly whisk from Tubuai in the Pacific Ocean, the President's whisk would be made with special care, out of attractive and valuable materials, woven, carved, and polished to make the most elegant impression.

Part of the Tubuai Islands, a small group of volcanic islands ringed with coral reefs that lies to the east of Australia, Tubuai came under the control of France in the nineteenth century and is now part of French Polynesia. As in all Pacific societies, social relationships based on gender, age, and ritual knowledge were important on Tubuai. These relationships were reflected in the objects people used. Particularly fine examples of everyday things owned by ordinary people – seats, articles of clothing and headgear, axes and fly whisks – were made for social leaders such as chiefs and priests.

## FLY WHISK

*Tubuai Islands, collected about 1825*

The Polynesian chief who owned this graceful fly whisk gave it up when his island was visited during the 1800s by ships from faraway countries that were exploring the islands dotted throughout the Pacific.

In the nearby Society Islands, most people carried whisks, particularly in places where food was being served or prepared, so their use probably had something to do with avoiding contamination. In addition to whisks or fans, the symbols of a chief's status traditionally included a special seat, a canoe, various utensils, weapons, and a feathered belt.

This whisk was transformed from being an everyday object into something special for an important owner. Almost three and a half feet in length, it is made of wood, plant fibers, feathers, and mother-of-pearl. Despite its length, it is extremely light in weight and so would be easy to wave about. So many textures were brought together to create one object! The dense fiber wrappings create a bumpy surface, while the jagged carving of the grip, bright density of the feathers, and soft opal-like sheen of the shell bring to mind different aspects of hardness, sharpness, and smoothness.

### AN ELEGANT HANDLE

The whisk has a carved wooden grip ending in a knob in the shape of two figures seated back-to-back, which may represent ancestors. Tightly twisted fibers wrapped around the handle below the grip fan out into a dense bunch of kinky strands from which flies would find it difficult to escape.

### WHAT IS THE WHISK MADE OF?

Locally available materials were used to make this object: plant fibers, a curved slice of mother-of-pearl, and red and yellow tufts that are probably feathers. In Polynesia, feathers were connected with the gods and were believed to convey sacredness to people who used objects decorated with them.

# Sweet Dreams of America

 THERE'S NOTHING NEW about recycling. In eighteenth- and nineteenth-century America, before there were shops that sold ready-made bed linen, women used to set aside colorful bits of fabric, lace, buttons, ribbons, and other trimmings to make their own bedcovers and quilts.

People kept materials to use again because they believed that nothing should be wasted, especially if it was cloth imported from faraway Europe and Asia, which was expensive. Handmade quilts and other types of bedcovers made by American women with no formal training are sometimes described as folk art. The methods they used were handed down from mother to daughter for generations. Many bedcovers like the one here are carefully preserved in museums or prized as family heirlooms. They tell us a lot about the hopes, dreams, and values of the women who made them.

The Centennial Exposition, held in 1876 to celebrate the hundredth anniversary of American independence, was probably one of the significant events in the lives of the two or three women who worked on this quilt. To mark the celebration, the quilters included squares showing buildings and emblems connected with the struggle for independence – including the Liberty Bell and Liberty Hall in Philadelphia, Pennsylvania – as well as the Memorial Hall and the Women's Pavilion at the exposition itself.

### CENTENNIAL ALBUM QUILT
*America, about 1876*

The women who created this colorful bedcover out of scraps of cotton cloth and silk were members of the Burdick-Childs family who may have lived in a small town in the state of Massachusetts. Figures of children and adults, an entire zoo of birds and animals, a variety of buildings – even silhouetted sea creatures and butterflies – all jostle for space within the grid of roughly twelve-and-a-half-inch squares.

### AN AFTERNOON OFF

A man and woman (perhaps
one of the quilters) have taken
their children to the park to play.
While the adults relax on a bench,
one child swings on a gate,
another retrieves his kite from
a tree, and a third is about to
throw a stick for a dog to fetch.
The trees have no leaves and
everyone is bundled up, so it must
be autumn – but with a twist:
the air is filled with butterflies.

The quilters also included scenes from closer
to home, and these give us a vivid sense of what life
was like in America at the time. They made it easy
for us to imagine what their town looked like, with
its houses, church steeples, and small businesses, and
the chickens, turkeys, and small animals people kept
in their backyards and gardens. They let us glimpse
inside their own homes: the quilt shows us shelves
filled with books, clocks, a tabletop globe, framed
portraits and mirrors, even a stuffed bird. We can see
a family having a meal, a boy reading, another boy
getting into mischief by climbing up on a chair.
We're reminded of how people got around: in
horse-drawn coaches, by bicycle, in canoes, aboard
sailing boats. To make the scenes as realistic as
possible, the quilters tried their hand at one–point
perspective and showed how things close to us look
bigger than things far away, no matter what size they
actually are. Some of the scenes and embroidered
quotes show us that they knew their Bible. They had
a sense of humor, too: while a man proposes
marriage in one square, kittens play in his upturned
top hat on the floor.

### A MORAL LESSON

A policeman in a brass-buttoned
blue coat is having words with
a shame-faced boy holding a hoe.
The row of farm animals – rabbits,
pigs, turkeys, a large guard dog –
suggests that the child is working
outdoors when he should be
improving his mind by attending
to his lessons inside the bright-red
school building.

The Centennial Album Quilt is a record
of several women's personal joy, their curiosity
about the world, their treasured memories,
their religious faith, and their social values.
It celebrates a nation's independence with
the same excitement as the smallest details of
family life, giving an overall impression
of exuberant celebration.

## CONTRASTING LANDSCAPES

The square on the left shows
a typical New England view:
a church behind a house. Beside
the house there's a warehouse with
barrels in the yard. In the next
square, above, we are in a different
world altogether. Bluebirds are
nesting in a ruined tower; a giraffe
saunters across a bridge. What
country is the hot-air balloon
flying over? Are those the Egyptian
pyramids in the background?
Could this be the quilter's vision
of the holy land?

## HOW WAS THE QUILT MADE?

The quilters collected the materials for their
masterpiece in a scrap bag. After looking through
prints and journals for inspiration, they made drawings
of the scenes they wanted to include. They chose the
fabric, and cut the pieces out carefully. Then they pinned
each piece onto its fabric background and sewed it in
place, using a technique called appliqué – French for
"applied" – and chain stitch. A completed quilt cover
would have been attached to a backing with a layer of
padding in between, and all three layers stitched
together to keep them in place.

# Joining the Community

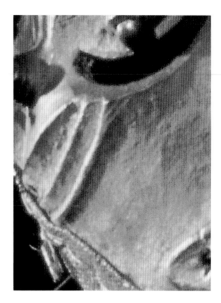

## IDENTIFYING MARKS

The three curving lines on each cheek of this mask represent cicatrices. Cicatrization – where the skin is cut and forms raised patterns as it heals – is one of the many forms of body adornment used in Central Africa. Patterns like these are thought to make people look more attractive.

WE ALL LIKE TO CELEBRATE special occasions. We look forward to the chance to dress up in our best clothes, and we bring out our favorite dishes, table decorations, and other accessories. But some special occasions stand out in another way, too: like weddings and funerals, these occasions mark moments in people's lives when they change status.

For the Pende people of Central Africa, the moment when a boy becomes a man is a very special occasion, marked by elaborate initiation rites. The ceremonies are organized by secret societies and associated with special artworks like the mask shown here.

To prepare for being "reborn" as adults, Pende boys spend some time living away from their community. They are taught songs, dances, and social values. (There are similar rituals for girls, but we know much less about them.) The boys are reintroduced into Pende society as grown-ups at a ceremonial masked dance. Most, if not all, of the dancers are male, although some pretend to be women, wearing masks representing the chief's wife, a seductive temptress, a beauty queen, and so on. Other masks represent important ancestors, nature spirits, and clowns. The dancers' bodies are always hidden beneath elaborate costumes.

The downcast eyes make this mask look sad, but there were cheerful and frightening masks, too. The eyebrows run in a line across the face, and there are cicatrices on the cheekbones. Air circulated between the mask and the dancer's face through the slits below the mask's eyes, the holes drilled into the nostrils, and the opening between the teeth. Dancers had to be able to breathe easily or they wouldn't have been able to move with speed and energy and provide exciting entertainment.

## MASK

*Pende, Democratic Republic
of the Congo, collected in 1910*

The type of wooden mask used
in ceremonies to initiate boys into
manhood was known as *mbuya*.
Try to imagine this one being
used in an elaborate, all-night
masquerade with music and singing,
and with lunging, jumping dancers
concealed inside elaborate costumes.

## HOW WAS THIS MASK MADE?

The Pende traditionally made
sculptures out of wood and ivory,
both of which were available locally.
The mask maker (always a man)
began by hacking out a rough shape
from a wooden block using an adze,
which is a type of axe; then he
carved the details with a knife.
The rough surface was smoothed
by rubbing it with sand
or coarse leaves. Fabrics and cords
were made of woven or twisted
raffia. Some of the materials used
in the masks and costumes were
perishable, so replacements had
to be made on a regular basis.
Few complete costumes survive.

71

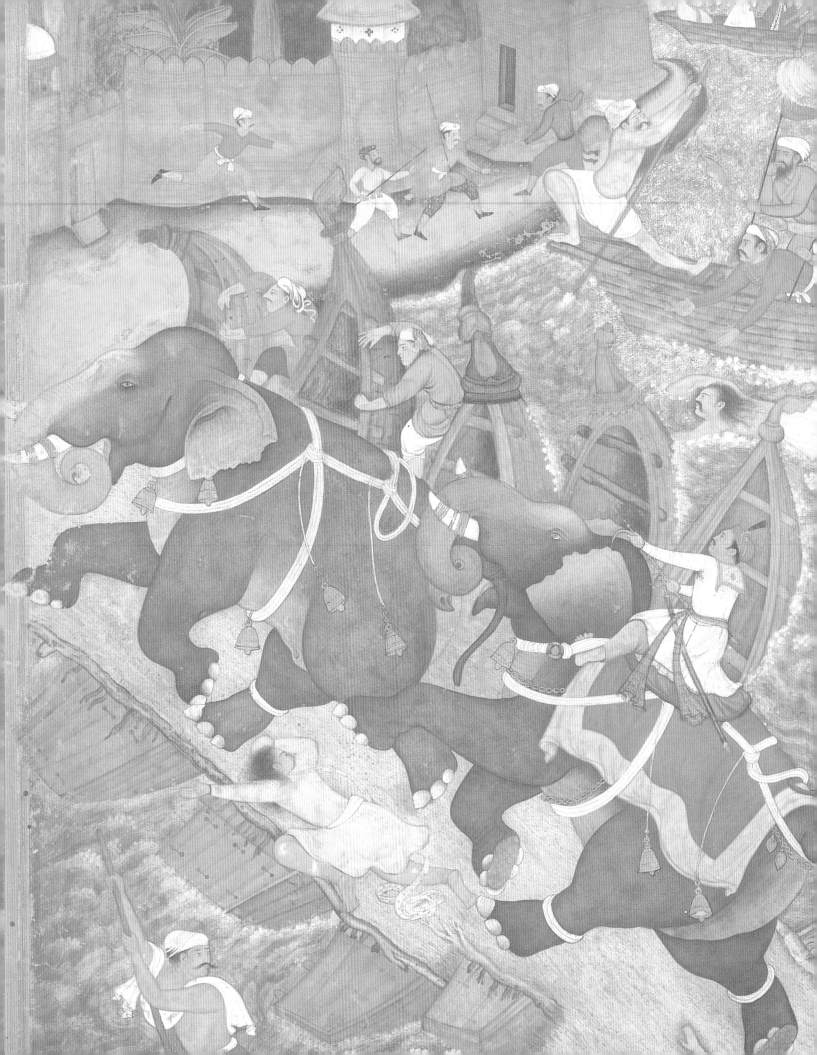

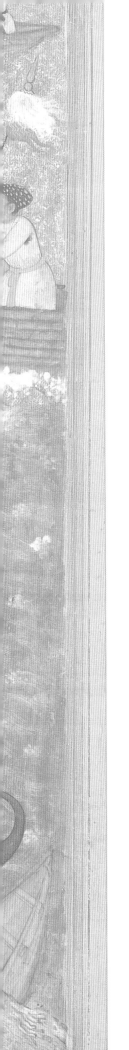
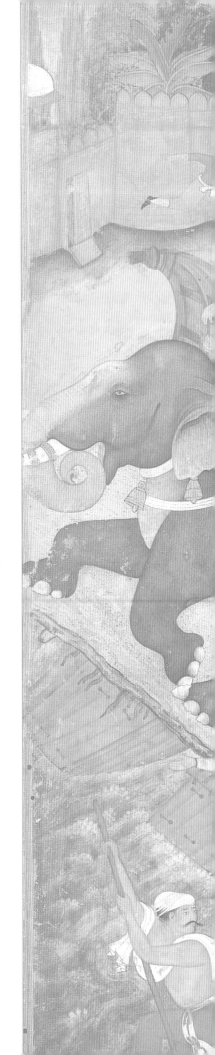

# History and Myth

# Monsters, Gods, and Heroes

 HERCULES, the star of a recent animated feature film, was not dreamt up by Hollywood filmmakers. Like Venus, Athena, and Zeus, he is one of a cast of goddesses, gods, heroes, and monsters whose colorful – sometimes outrageous – exploits are brought to life in the myths of ancient Greece.

Greek storytellers made up these tales of ambition, war, tragedy, passion, jealousy, patience, and disappointment more than twenty-five hundred years ago. The characters in them range from the loftiest heavenly beings down to the most miserable earthly creatures – some of the monsters rival those in *Star Wars*. Greek artists painted scenes from these stories on a wide range of vases whose curved surfaces challenged their skill and ingenuity.

In the seventh century B.C., Greek craftsmen invented a technique known as black-figure painting, showing silhouetted figures against pale backgrounds, with cut-in lines for details. The potter who made this drinking cup – known as a kylix – added reddish pigment to make the colors warmer. He must have known every detail of the myth about Bellerophon and his winged horse, Pegasus, and although he had only a small area to work on – a circle of nearly five inches across – he managed to give their meeting with the horrific Chimera great impact. The struggling bodies of the horse and the monster form an arch. Beneath them crouches a tiny-headed, huge-thighed figure: it's Bellerophon, focused and calm as he delivers the death thrust.

## BLACK-FIGURED KYLIX
*Greece, 570-565 B.C.*

In order to prove that he had been wrongly accused of a crime, the hero Bellerophon set out to kill the Chimera, a flame-breathing lion with a goat's head on its back and a snake as its tail. Here, a moment of high drama is captured on a tiny surface. Bellerophon rams his spear into the monster's belly, while his horse, Pegasus, strikes the lion head with his hooves. Defeated, the Chimera turns away, its tongue lolling in pain.

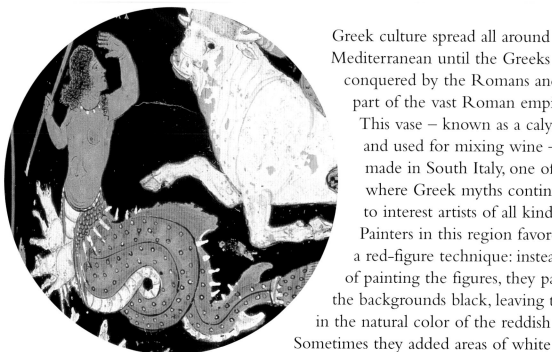

Greek culture spread all around the Mediterranean until the Greeks were conquered by the Romans and made part of the vast Roman empire.

This vase – known as a calyx-krater and used for mixing wine – was made in South Italy, one of the areas where Greek myths continued to interest artists of all kinds. Painters in this region favored a red-figure technique: instead of painting the figures, they painted the backgrounds black, leaving the figures in the natural color of the reddish clay. Sometimes they added areas of white or highlights for a livelier atmosphere. Asteas, the painter who created this scene of Europa being carried off to the island of Crete, set it within an archway, separating the players in the drama into earthly and heavenly zones: six gods and goddesses look down on the scene as if from the balcony of a theater. A parade of winged griffins chase each other around the foot of the vase, above a garland of vine leaves with waving tendrils. Greek artists often used repeating patterns in bands or borders like these.

## A WATERY WORLD

Asteas shows us Zeus carrying Europa away across a sea filled with fish. Triton and Scylla accompany them. Triton was the son of the god of the sea. The sea nymph Scylla, shown above, suffered a horrible fate at the hands of a jealous goddess, who changed the lower half of her body into a fish tail, with a belt made of the heads of hideous dogs around her waist.

### RED-FIGURED CALYX-KRATER

*Asteas, South Italy, about 340 B.C.*

This imposing vase with a flaring lip and great curved
handles is almost three and a half feet tall. It illustrates a
scene from Greek mythology: a princess named Europa
being carried off from the seaside by Zeus, the king of the
gods, who is disguised for the occasion as a white bull.
Precariously balanced, Europa clings to the bull's neck,
struggling to keep her veil under control, more concerned
about how she looks than where she is going. As he
gallops along, the bull turns his head to fix us with one
black eye, as if to see if we appreciate his cleverness.

# Long Live the King!

THE YORUBA PEOPLES of southwestern Nigeria tell of a High God who sent several less-important gods down from the heavens on an iron chain to create the world. One of these lesser gods, Oduduwa, founded the city of Ife in southwestern Nigeria and became its first *Oni*, or king. While Ife went on to become an important trading center, Oduduwa's children, who left the city to found kingdoms of their own throughout Yorubaland, are remembered today as the Yoruba's semidivine ancestors.

This head of an *Oni* was probably made about eight hundred years ago. When sculptures like it were discovered by archaeologists in Nigeria during the 1930s, the *Oni* at the time took a great deal of interest in them. He stopped some of the archaeologists' work because he did not want to have the bones of the royal family's ancestors disturbed.

Most of the metal Ife heads like this one are life-size. The parallel lines covering the face probably represent scarifications – regularly patterned scars – and help to focus our attention on the softly rounded contours of the *Oni's* skin. The small, almond-shaped eyes, straight nose, and full lips suggest that this *Oni* was a thoughtful person, perhaps a bit sad. Originally, the head might have been attached to a wooden body. The entire figure could have been used in a special ceremony following the *Oni's* funeral to show that the power of Yoruba kingship survived despite the death of a particular king.

## A ROYAL EMBLEM

Although *Oni*s wore many different types of crowns, all of them – like this one – have a cone-shaped ornament above the forehead with a finial that looks like a lit candle. The rows of holes where the *Oni's* moustache and beard would have been – which you can see in the main picture – may be where real hair was fastened to the sculpture to enhance its lifelike appearance.

## IFE KING (ONI)
*Nigeria, 12th century*

This bronze portrait of one of the *Onis*, or kings, of the city of Ife presents its subject as calm, strong, and self-confident. Yoruba artisans of the time created sculptures of animals and humans from terra-cotta and metal, using sophisticated casting techniques to work with copper, brass, and bronze. Very few heads like this one have survived.

79

# The Game of Love

THE PEOPLE OF AZERBAIJAN in Central Asia think of Ilyas ibn Yusuf Nizami as their national hero.

Nizami lived in a valley in the rugged Caucasus Mountains eight hundred years ago. He was the author of the *Khamsa*, a set of five epic poems written in the Persian language, which inspired artists throughout the Islamic world. One of these poems – "Khusraw and Shirin" – tells the story of Khusraw, the dashing prince who ruled Persia (present-day Iran) in the sixth century A.D.

According to Nizami, Khusraw fell in love with an Armenian princess named Shirin who enjoyed hunting and playing sports. So, supported by their companions, the prince and princess had a game of polo. Polo, which was probably invented in Persia, is a demanding and dangerous sport, still played by princes today. Polo ponies have to be extremely fit; there is plenty of swerving and twisting, and riders often lean right off their saddles to make a shot.

The players galloping toward each other just below the brow of the hill are Khusraw and Shirin: they have the largest horses and wear elaborate feathered turbans or crowns as befits a prince and princess. They grip their reins and lean forward eagerly to engage with the ball, their mallets marking an uneven "X" on the blossoming hillside. The artist placed the ball exactly in the middle of the picture as if to draw our attention to the struggle between the two lovers: whoever managed to control the ball would win the match. Who would it be – Khusraw and his courtiers, or Shirin with her ladies-in-waiting?

## A REAL KING

Prince Khusraw was more than just a romantic hero: he became Shah Khusraw Parwiz of Persia, famous for his reforms of the Persian government. He modeled his new system of taxation on that of ancient Rome.

## HOW WAS THE MANUSCRIPT ARRANGED?

Rather than separating the texts from their illustrations, many Persian manuscripts bring words and pictures together. The panels of text here read right to left. The one that runs across the bottom of the picture acts like a safety barrier separating us from the game in progress.

## A MINIATURE DEPICTING A GAME OF POLO
*Persia, 16th century*

Thundering hooves and the whoosh and crack of wooden mallets arcing through the air and glancing off one another: a moment of high drama is shown in this lively illustration from one of medieval Persia's great epic poems.

# Akbar and the Runaway Elephant

IF CAMERAS HAD BEEN INVENTED in the sixteenth century, this episode from the life of the Mughal emperor Akbar would have provided a front-page photo for the Indian newspapers.

Instead, Akbar had a painting of it made by Basawan, one of his favorite artists. This miniature was given a special place in Akbar's own luxurious copy of the *Akbarnama*. The illuminations in this book give some idea of the Mughal court's magnificence and of Akbar's dynamism and courage.

The elephant Hawa'i ("Sky Rocket") was known for his fierceness. Although elephant drivers found it difficult to control him, Akbar (then only nineteen) climbed onto Sky Rocket's back. With Akbar urging him on, Sky Rocket won a fight with another elephant, who then took off with Sky Rocket in hot pursuit. Chaos resulted when the two beasts thundered across a floating bridge that was unstable at the best of times.

Whether Basawan witnessed the event or not, he created an action-filled painting that crackles with excitement, suggesting the unsteadiness of the moment by setting the bridge at a sharp diagonal. The pontoons seem about to slide away into the river; a man's turban has completely unraveled; lively figures run back and forth along the far bank in confusion.

But Basawan also made sure to include details that anchor us in everyday reality: curved daggers tucked safely into belts, cords knotted carefully over the elephants' backs, the scaly bottoms of Sky Rocket's huge feet. Just as Akbar gave balance and stability to his empire, Basawan set precision at the center of a chaotic world.

## COOL, CALM, AND COLLECTED

Akbar appears totally at ease in the face of catastrophe. With one foot tucked under Sky Rocket's harness, he guides the maddened beast with effortless assurance, the picture of a ruler in complete control of his destiny.

## WHO WAS BASAWAN?

One of the most famous artists of Akbar's time, Basawan contributed to all of the illustrated manuscripts created in the imperial workshops over a period of forty years.

## AKBAR TAMES THE SAVAGE ELEPHANT

*Basawan, Mughal Empire, about 1590*

This is the left half of an illustrated pair of facing pages from
the *Akbarnama*, the sixteenth-century biography of the Mughal emperor
Akbar written by Shaykh Abu'l-Fazl. Painted in gouache on paper,
the scene shows the teenage emperor subduing a wild elephant.

83

## PUPPET

*Java, about 1900*

Javanese shadow puppets like
this one are made of wood,
carved in shallow relief,
and sheets of buffalo leather,
painted in bright colors.
They are controlled by rods
attached to their hands, and their
elbows and shoulders are hinged
so that they can be made
to move and gesture.

# The Asthmatic Prince

THE LONGEST POEM IN THE WORLD is the *Mahabharata*. It has more than sixty characters, including gods, kings, priests, knights, princesses, demons, servants, and animals. One of the characters is a cunning, fast-talking prince who has asthma. His name is Patih Harja Sakuni.

This shadow puppet of Harja Sakuni once belonged to a puppet master on Java, one of the islands of Indonesia. Javanese puppeteers have been retelling episodes from the *Mahabharata* for a thousand years. The story of Harja Sakuni begins with his attempt to win a competition to marry the daughter of the king of Madura. A rival, Prince Dastarastra, wins instead. When Harja Sakuni tries to run away with the princess, Dastarastra defeats him in battle. Later on in the great Hindu saga, the wily asthmatic prince meets a particularly nasty end in a great war.

Javanese puppeteers sit on the ground with small groups of musicians, making the shadow puppets sing, speak, and move, sometimes against a white screen lit from behind so that they cast a shadow. Performances last for hours; the audience drifts in and out. A good puppet master must memorize complicated stories and know each character's personality, postures, and ways of speaking. He needs to be able to speak several dialects, sing well, and know how to perform the rituals and prayers associated with shadow-puppet performances.

So, on top of everything else, that makes the puppet master a kind of priest. Since one side of the theater is thought to be positive and the other negative, and the plays are about the struggle between positive and negative forces in the universe – good and evil – the dramas have a cosmic meaning. Particular episodes from these ancient stories are performed to protect children born at certain times of the year or to honor the dead. Paid for by members of the royal court and villagers alike, the puppet plays connect the Javanese to their ancient past.

### A PARTICULAR PRINCE

A puppet master might have two hundred puppets in his collection, so he has to be able to tell them apart easily. Harja Sakuni is recognizable by his bulging eye, enormous nose and nasty grimace; his diadem (crown) with its long "tail"; and his hunched shoulders, which suggest that he has difficulty breathing.

### WHAT IS THE *MAHABHARATA*?

Written in India over several centuries, this epic saga describes the tragic feud between two branches of a Hindu royal family, and the events that finally result in a war of truly catastrophic proportions.

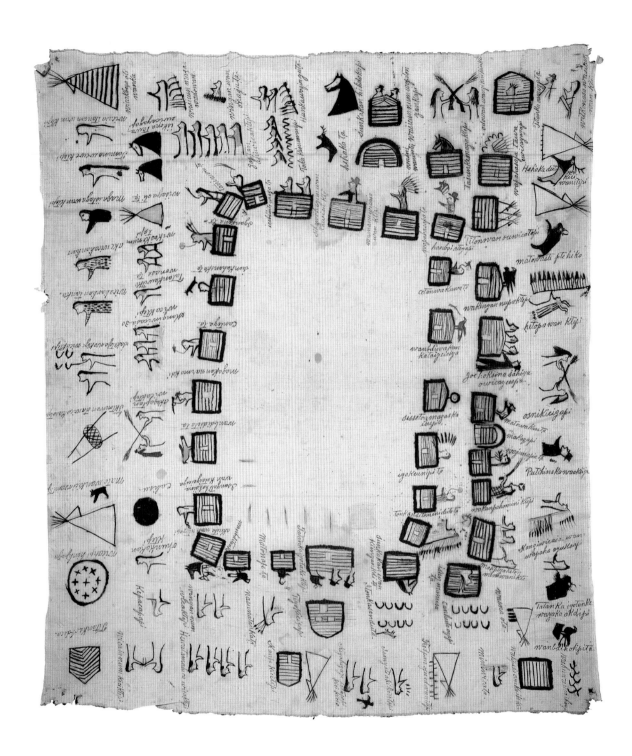

## SIOUX WINTER COUNT

*Fort Totten Reservation, North Dakota, 1900-15*

This Winter Count – a large rectangle of cotton cloth
covered with images of Native American life drawn
in ink and various pigments – chronicles the history
of a group of Sioux at the turn of the century.

# A Spiral of Years

THE SIOUX OF AMERICA'S GREAT PLAINS recorded their history using the world's oldest form of writing: pictographs – simplified outline drawings whose meanings are instantly recognizable.

The Sioux lived in small bands, hunting buffalo and moving from place to place between the Mississippi River and the Rocky Mountains. Hunting and waging war were the two most important activities for Sioux men. The pictographic records they painted on large buffalo hides or pieces of cloth show their horses; the buffalo, deer and birds they hunted; the homes – tipis – where they lived with their families; their weapons (especially rifles); their chiefs, who wore elaborate feather headdresses; and the number of enemies they had killed.

This painted cloth, about three and a half feet wide by more than three and a half feet long, represents the Winter Count kept by a single Sioux group between 1823 and 1911. A Winter Count was a history in pictures, organized like a calendar. Each winter, the keeper of the Count and members of the group chose one event to stand for the year just passed. This event was represented by a pictograph. Over the years, the keeper arranged these pictographs in rows or, as here, in a spiral. (This one begins at the bottom right corner and proceeds inward.) Winter Counts were meant to help people remember both their personal history and the history of their tribe.

Each pictograph has a caption, which was probably added later. Only very significant happenings, such as outbreaks of deadly illness, major conflicts, and dramatic natural events were considered important enough to stand for specific years. For example, a dreadful smallpox epidemic is recorded on the upper left-hand edge by two figures whose bodies are covered in spots.

### FALLING STARS

The pictograph for the year 1833, captioned "the stars fell," is a circle filled with small crosses. In November that year, there was a spectacular meteor shower, an event recorded in another Sioux Winter Count as the "storm-of-stars-winter."

**87**

# The Magical Breadfruit Tree

IN SOCIETIES WITHOUT WRITING, people learn about their past by listening to their elders tell stories. The people of Belau in the Pacific Ocean have handed down their history in this way for centuries. The most important stories are about wars, relationships between women and men, and extraordinary events such as encounters with gods and monsters. Episodes from these tales are carved on wooden planks used in the building of *bai* – community centers where councils and clubs can get together for meetings.

All *bai* are decorated, but those belonging to chiefs are the most elaborate. Historically, the boards were also painted in red, yellow, black, and white ochres (earth-based pigments).

The tale of a magical breadfruit tree appears on many *bai* storyboards. A woman called Dirabkau, who lives alone on a coral island, discovers a child in an egg. She calls him Terkelel and raises him as her own. When he asks her why she eats nothing but breadfruit rather than fish from the sea like the other islanders, she explains that she's always been poor

and had to get by on her own – without a husband
or any help from her neighbors. Terkelel makes a hole
in the breadfruit tree so that water from the sea sloshes
up through its trunk, bringing fish with it. Dirabkau's
neighbors are filled with envy that she should get fish
without having to work for it like they do. They cut down
the tree – creating a gap through which the sea rushes in,
flooding the island. Everyone is drowned except Dirabkau
and her son.

The storyboard shows everything happening at once.
At the right, Dirabkau (wearing a skirt) has just caught a
fish has tossed up by the sea through the trunk of
the magical tree. Between Dirabkau and the tree is
an angry neighbor brandishing an axe, ready to cut the
tree down. At the left, there is a man on a raft who may
be Terkelel, rushing to save his mother from the flood.

### FREE DELIVERY

In Belau, fishing was traditionally
a man's job. Dirabkau had no
husband, so she had no one
to fish for her and nothing to eat
but breadfruit. When Terkelel
arranged for his mother to have
an endless supply of fish without
having to lift a finger, the other
islanders were furious.

### STORYBOARD OF THE
### MAGICAL BREADFRUIT TREE
*Belau, collected about 1948*

This storyboard is made of painted wood. It
illustrates a story told in Belau, a small group
of islands in the Pacific Ocean east of the
Philippines. The characters are a lone parent,
her adopted son, their envious neighbors,
and a special evergreen tree.

89

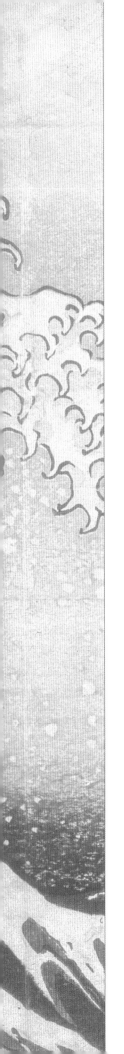
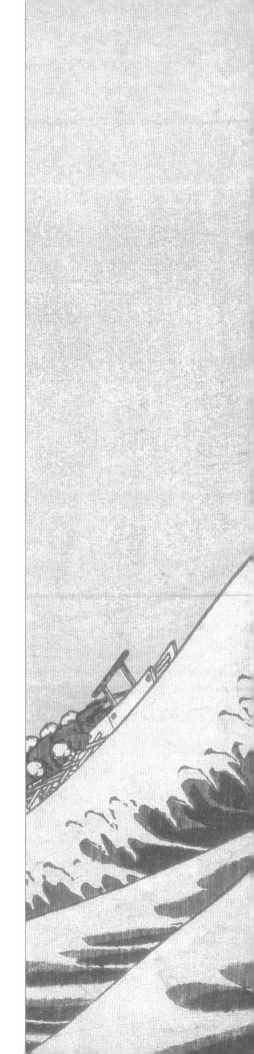

# World of Nature

# Art on the Land

### ROCK PAINTING

*Cueva de las Manos, Patagonia, Argentina, date unknown*

On the pitted surface of a rock shelter in South America, two prints of human hands are surrounded by dots, streaks, and splashes of red paint. A herd of wild llamas, with spindly legs and graceful necks, scatter in all directions.

SOME ARTISTS IN THE MOST ANCIENT OF TIMES used the landscapes around them as their canvases. They scratched, painted, pressed, and scraped patterns and scenes onto rocky outcroppings or the walls and ceilings of hidden caves. Today, these markings and pictures are known as rock art.

It isn't clear why rock artists chose the sites they did. Some were linked to trails, while others may have been used for rituals. The meanings of rock paintings are often

unclear, too. It is impossible to know what the llama meant to the person who painted this galloping herd. Were llamas, native to the Andes, hunted for food? Maybe they had already been tamed to carry heavy burdens.

The two handprints were made using red pigment: one by applying it to the palm and then pressing directly onto the rock, and the other by blowing or spraying powdered pigment around a hand to create an eerie result – a pale silhouette captured in a wild red halo.

## HANDS UP!

The human hand is a powerful symbol in many cultures. Clusters of stenciled hands, sometimes hundreds of them, have been found in rock shelters in Patagonia, a region of Argentina at the foot of the Andes Mountains. We don't know what the motif means. Perhaps, like graffiti, it was a way of announcing "I was here" in paint.

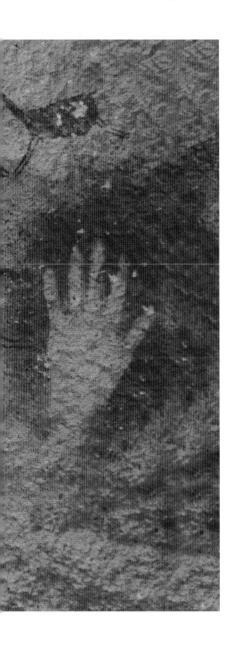

### HOW WAS ROCK ART MADE?

Rock artists used several different techniques. They cut lines and patterns into rocks with sharp tools and used flints for scratching and scraping. Charcoal and locally available ground-up mineral pigments were used for painting with fingers, fiber "brushes," wood splinters, and bristles, or for "blowing," sometimes through tubes. Paints would seep into stony surfaces, so when the water or binder they were mixed with evaporated, they became part of the rock, surviving for thousands of years.

# Paradise on Earth

THE OTTOMAN SULTANS who ruled Turkey after the collapse of the Byzantine empire were not just fierce soldiers, inspired politicians, and dedicated patrons of architecture and the arts; they were enthusiastic gardeners, too.

Among the elegant buildings that make up the Topkapi Palace overlooking Istanbul's Golden Horn (its famous harbor), the Ottomans created gardens with pathways and fountains, and gracious pavilions with shady seats from which to admire the spectacular views of the city. As Muslims, the Ottomans believed in the Prophet Mohammed's promise that all believers would one day enter paradise. Covering bare ground with trees and flowers and guiding water through the dry, rugged landscape beautified the environment and provided a refuge from heat and dust. It was also a way of reminding people of the Prophet's promise.

## DISH

*Turkey, about 1550*

When Turkey was ruled by the Ottoman sultans, the small town of Iznik, southeast of Istanbul, became a center for producing brightly colored ceramic tiles, jars, tankards, bowls, and hanging lamps. Like this large, shallow bowl, many Iznik pieces feature the flowers favored by Ottoman gardeners, painted in blue, turquoise, purple, olive green, and gray.

Plant motifs were important in the decoration of Islamic buildings, and many ceramic tiles and lamps were covered with flowers. During the Ottoman period, the workshops of Iznik developed a special ceramic style based on floral forms, one or two types of trees, Arabic calligraphy, and a small number of geometric patterns. The Ottoman sultans ordered tiles for their mosques and palaces from Iznik, but the workshops also made ceramics for everyday use like this generously sized bowl.

Here the decorator focused on a graceful bouquet, including four drooping, dark-blue tulips, graceful stems of pale-purple hyacinths and prunus, and a single, small blue carnation (at the bottom left). The three large, two-toned blossoms are difficult to identify, since, unlike the other flowers, they're not especially realistic. Their leaves suggest that they're roses or peonies. The stems are fastened with a scalloped turquoise ring and fluttering blue ribbons – a bouquet with a joyous message from a part of the world where gardens are thought of as paradise on earth.

### SURROUNDED BY WATER

These painted whirls, interrupted along both edges by white paw-like shapes, represent rushing water; the "paws" are whitecaps breaking over the surface – a burbling stream framing a flowery offering.

### WHERE DO TULIPS COME FROM?

Tulips were unknown outside Turkey until the middle of the sixteenth century, when a European ambassador noticed them growing there. Imported seeds and bulbs produced beautiful, unscented flowers that astonished German and Flemish botanists. When it became clear that plant collectors and gardeners would do anything to get their hands on these exotic plants, their prices soared. During the seventeenth century, Dutch speculators made and lost fortunes trading in tulips, which are commonplace in European gardens and florist shops today.

# Like an Enchantment

IMAGINE HOW YOU'D FEEL, after months on board ship, when you finally arrived at a world totally different from your own: a beautiful but hostile environment populated by a baffling array of plants and creatures.

The young midshipman George Raper must have experienced fear, excitement, wide-eyed curiosity, and utter disbelief when he arrived in Australia in 1788 aboard the *Sirius. Sirius* was the flagship of the First Fleet, which brought convicts from England to set up a colony on the southeastern coast of what was then an unknown and mysterious continent to Europeans.

Within a short time, Raper was making a painted record of what he observed there, including animals like the "kangooroo," shown in this watercolor in front of a gum tree (a fast-growing evergreen native to Australia but now grown all over the world). As the colony grew, Raper recorded its changing appearance, including a view of the governor's imposing house near what is now Sydney's bustling harbor.

To convicts who were shipped there against their will, Australia represented the ultimate punishment; to others, it seemed like paradise. Judging from his careful, gently respectful kangaroo portrait, Raper must have shared the wonderment of another newly arrived Englishman, who noted in his diary that the air, filled with the songs of outrageously plumed birds, seemed "like an enchantment."

### FRIEND OR FOE?

Perhaps because he was unable to get close enough to the kangaroo to study it properly, Raper made its head look more like that of an alert dog - with big, liquid eyes; long lashes; thick, stubby ears; and a generous sprinkling of whiskers.

### GUM-PLANT AND KANGOOROO OF NEW HOLLAND
*George Raper, Australia, 1789*

The naval officer George Raper was one of the first European artists to paint a kangaroo, shown here in delicate shades of watercolor and ink against a flat, barren landscape and huge, open sky.

### WHAT IS A MARSUPIAL?

Kangaroos, like koala bears, opossums, and wombats, are marsupials: mammals whose young are born before they are fully formed. To protect them until they can forage for themselves, adult marsupials carry their babies around in pouches.

# Chaos and Calm

FORCES OF NATURE beyond human control make exciting subjects. When the Japanese printmaker Hokusai created this powerful image of an enormous wave threatening three fragile boats, he succeeded in capturing nature's violent and tranquil aspects in one beautifully balanced picture.

*The Great Wave* is probably the most famous Japanese print ever made. It comes from a series called *Thirty-six Views of Mount Fuji*. In Hokusai's time, Mount Fuji – a dormant volcano 12,388 feet high – could be seen from the city of Edo on a clear day, even though it was almost 100 miles away. In this print series, Hokusai explored the changing aspects of the volcano, which had been sacred to the Japanese for centuries.

Three slender wooden boats, each manned by eight straining rowers, struggle not to be smashed to smithereens as they head straight into a monstrous wave. The wave is so threatening, and the danger so clear, that towering, snow-capped Fuji is reduced to a tiny toy volcano, framed by the water's toboggan curve. Fearsome in reality and miles away from the sea, the mountain has become part of the seascape, its white peak a beacon of serenity untouched by the wave's frothy claws.

Hokusai linked the violent sea and unmoving mountain by using very few colors: two shades of blue ink (one almost black) and a range of pale tones for the sky and boats. In this way, he expressed the balance that exists between peace and danger in the natural world.

### WILL THEY MAKE IT?

Hokusai has given us no clues at all as to whether the boatmen will get safely back to port, unless Fuji's presence suggests that dry land is close by – if they can just hang on to their courage and ride the great wave.

## WHO WAS HOKUSAI?

Japan's most famous artist, Hokusai was
an unusually active man. In ninety years,
he changed his name more than thirty times,
moved his home more than ninety times,
and produced 30,000 designs for prints,
as well as a number of novels and poems.

## THE GREAT WAVE

*Katsushika Hokusai, Japan, about 1830*

Hokusai's woodblock print *The Great Wave*,
from the first series of large-scale landscape prints
to be published in Edo (present-day Kyoto),
went through many printings and has become
one of the most famous images in world art.

# Natural Wonders

IN 1831, AROUND THE TIME this postcard-sized ceramic plaque was made in Derby, England, Charles Darwin set sail for South America on the *HMS Beagle*. His aim was to discover a way to fit the world's wonders into one all-embracing vision of creation.

Like Darwin, European artists of the early 1800s, especially ceramists and jewelers, were fascinated by the tiny details that enable us to distinguish one species of animal, bird, or insect from all the others. They often highlighted these differences in their work, celebrating nature's apparently endless variety.

Some ceramic artisans even sculpted three-dimensional insects, lizards, snakes, and sea creatures that perch on teapot lids, climb up vases, or slither across the insides of serving dishes.

Sampson Hancock treated the bee, butterflies, moths, and ladybirds on this small plaque like study specimens, setting their colorful variety against a pale background and making sure that each one was both scientifically accurate and easy to see. The large black, white, and rust-colored butterfly near the center of the plaque is a Red Admiral. There are Garden Tiger and Magpie moths just below the two top corners and a Small Copper moth at the left-hand edge. Hancock's celebration of their fragile perfection is successful both as a scientific document and as a delightful work of decorative art.

## SUMMER VIEWING

You might see Garden Tiger moths flitting around the house or streetlights in the middle of summer. They have wingspans of about two and a half inches, and their bright-orange abdomens and underwings decorated with black dots and stripes make them easy to spot. Their elegant forewings, patterned in cream and velvety black, might make you think of zebras or leopards.

## PORCELAIN PLAQUE
## HAND-PAINTED WITH BUTTERFLIES
*Sampson Hancock, England, about 1830*

Porcelain is a translucent ceramic that is usually white. It was invented in China and copied throughout Europe and the Near East. The town of Derby, where Hancock worked, was a center for the production of porcelain from the 1750s. Hancock must have had a print, watercolor, or collection of specimens to work from.

## IRISES

*Vincent van Gogh, Netherlands, 1889*

Born in Holland in 1853 into a family of pastors
and picture dealers, van Gogh was a deeply
troubled man who believed passionately in
the sacredness of art and nature. This belief
inspired this close-up view of a bunch of irises and
marigolds crowded into the corner of a sunny
French garden.

# Painting and Planting

GARDENS FILLED WITH FLOWERS and bright summer sunshine inspired two of the most famous painters in history to create some of their most well-known pictures.

Although Vincent van Gogh wanted to become a preacher, once he began to paint and draw he found he couldn't stop. After trying to work in Paris, he moved to the south of France. There he spent time in a hospital recuperating after an illness, possibly epilepsy. The hospital had a garden, and that was where he painted *Irises*. Although van Gogh thought of this picture as a study on which to base further work, rather than a finished painting, it contains so much energy that the flowers practically jump off the canvas. The deep purple irises wobble and bob about, their stems and long, strappy leaves dancing and twisting, like underwater plants swaying beneath the waves, or a crowd of marchers jostling along in a holiday parade.

The white iris off to the left stands out from the others, bold or hesitant, depending on how you interpret it. Perhaps van Gogh had his own changing moods in mind when he painted it.

## ORIENTAL INFLUENCE

Like other European artists of his time, van Gogh was fascinated by the art of Japan. His choice of irises as a subject, his use of flat areas of color and thick, dark outlines, and his arrangement of this picture like a flat screen may have been suggested by the Japanese woodblock prints he collected.

## WHAT IS A STUDY?

European painters with traditional training kept records in the form of sketched or painted patterns and details, assembling these into finished pictures on canvas or board in their workshops or studios. Known as studies, these sketches were meant as visual diary entries, not for exhibition or sale.

**OPTICAL ILLUSIONS**

Seen close up, the blobs, streaks and spots of colour in *The Water-Lily Pond* vibrate like pulsing lights or stars swimming in the night sky. It's not at all clear what these markings are meant to represent until you step back and look at the picture as a whole.

Van Gogh's devoted brother Theo bought and sold pictures for a living. One of the painters whose work he sold was Claude Monet, the most famous of the Impressionists. Monet was almost as passionate about gardening as he was about painting. "What I need most of all," he said when he was eighty years old, "are flowers." Monet created his gardens at Giverny as if he were painting with plants, building, among other features, an arching Japanese bridge over a water-lily pond. Monet liked to paint the same subjects again and again, at different times and in changing conditions; this is one of eighteen views he painted of his water garden. Unlike van Gogh's rowdy close-up, Monet's view is calm and centered; its blues, greens, pinks, and grays hum gently like lazy bees, giving us an impression of balance, warmth, and safety. Instead of floating, the lilies hover just above the water's surface; the pond seems both deep and flat, like a mirror; and it's difficult to say where the reflections end and the actual plants begin. Stunned by the heat, we can't tell exactly what we are seeing, but, whispers Monet, in this magic space it doesn't really matter.

**WHO WERE THE IMPRESSIONISTS?**

The French Impressionists were a group of nineteenth-century artists who tried to capture the effects of changing light and weather on their subjects. In the beginning art critics laughed at them, particularly since their brightly colored pictures looked sketchy and unfinished.

**THE WATER-LILY POND**
*Claude Monet, France, 1899*

After he became rich and successful as the champion of an entirely new way of painting, Monet purchased a large estate at Giverny, near Paris. The water garden he created there inspired much of his later work, including this picture of a bridge amid luxurious plantings. Some of the canvases Monet painted of the water garden were so huge that he had to build a special studio to work on them.

# Where Do the Objects Come From?

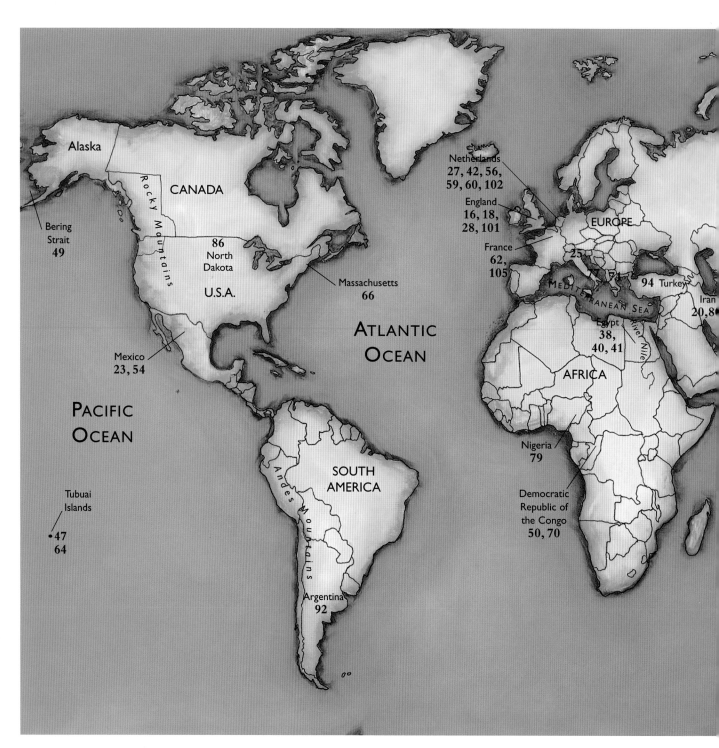

Alaska

CANADA

Rocky Mountains

Bering
Strait
**49**

**86**
North
Dakota

U.S.A.

Massachusetts
**66**

Mexico
**23, 54**

PACIFIC
OCEAN

ATLANTIC
OCEAN

Tubuai
Islands

•**47**
**64**

Andes Mountains

SOUTH
AMERICA

Argentina
**92**

Netherlands
**27, 42, 56,
59, 60, 102**

England
**16, 18,
28, 101**

France
**62,
105**

EUROPE

25

MEDITERRANEAN SEA

**94** Turkey

Iran
**20, 8**

Egypt
**38,
40, 41**

River Nile

AFRICA

Nigeria
**79**

Democratic
Republic of
the Congo
**50, 70**

# Key

**p.16**
Psalter world map

**p.18**
The Crystal Palace Game

**p.20**
Pen box

**p.23**
Calendar stone

**p.25**
Ship-shaped clock

**p.27**
*Still Life*

**p.28**
*Galloping*

**p.30**
*Bush Banana Dreaming*

**p.34**
Bronze *zun*

**p.36**
Bronze *hu*

**p.38**
*Book of the Dead*

**p.40**
Wooden coffin and mummy

**p.41**
*Shabti* box

**p.42**
*The Annunciation*

**p.45**
Conch-shell trumpet

**p.47**
The God A'a

**p.49**
Transformation mask

**p.50**
*Nkondi* statue

**p.54**
Stone lintel

**p.56**
*The Arnolfini Marriage*

**p.59**
*The Magdalen Reading*

**p.60**
The "Golf Book"

**p.62**
*Before the Ball*

**p.64**
Fly whisk

**p.66**
Centennial album quilt

**p.71**
Pende mask

**p.74**
Black-figured kylix

**p.77**
Red-figured calyx-krater

**p.79**
Ife King *(Oni)*

**p.80**
Persian manuscript

**p.83**
*Akbarnama*

**p.84**
Shadow puppet

**p.86**
Sioux winter count

**p.88**
The Magical Breadfruit Tree

**p.92**
Rock painting

**p.94**
Iznik dish

**p.96**
*Gum-plant and Kangooroo*

**p.99**
*The Great Wave*

**p.101**
Plaque of butterflies

**p.102**
*Irises*

**p.105**
*The Water-Lily Pond*

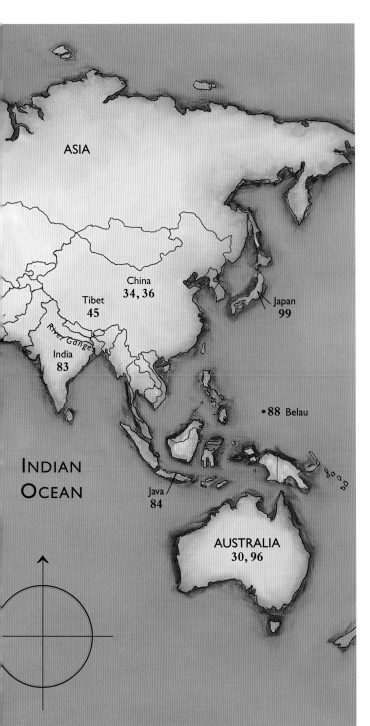

ASIA

China
**34, 36**

Tibet
**45**

River Ganges

India
**83**

Japan
**99**

•**88** Belau

INDIAN OCEAN

Java
**84**

AUSTRALIA
**30, 96**

# How Old Are the Objects?

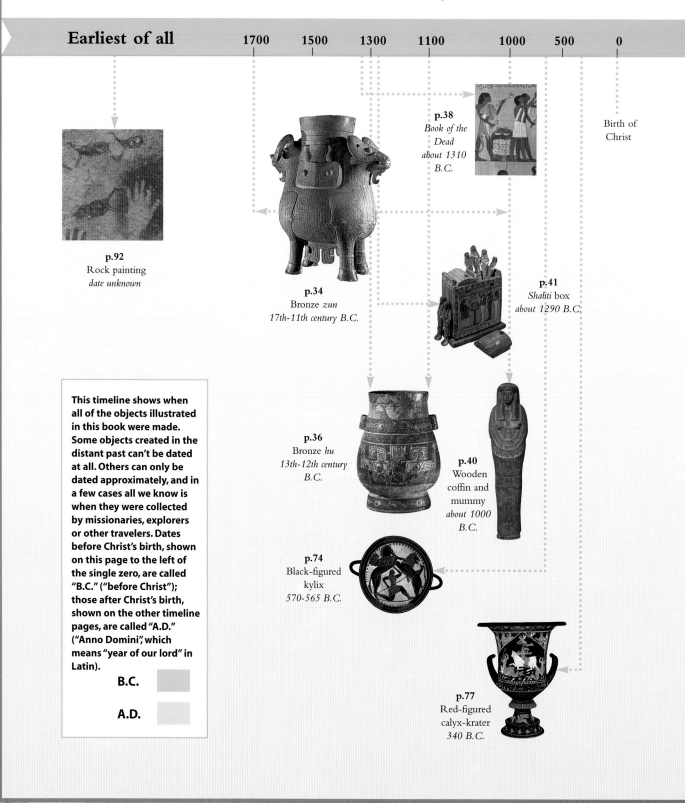

**Earliest of all**   1700   1500   1300   1100   1000   500   0

Birth of
Christ

**p.38**
*Book of the
Dead
about 1310
B.C.*

**p.92**
Rock painting
*date unknown*

**p.34**
Bronze *zun*
*17th-11th century B.C.*

**p.41**
*Shabti* box
*about 1290 B.C.*

This timeline shows when
all of the objects illustrated
in this book were made.
Some objects created in the
distant past can't be dated
at all. Others can only be
dated approximately, and in
a few cases all we know is
when they were collected
by missionaries, explorers
or other travelers. Dates
before Christ's birth, shown
on this page to the left of
the single zero, are called
"B.C." ("before Christ");
those after Christ's birth,
shown on the other timeline
pages, are called "A.D."
("Anno Domini", which
means "year of our lord" in
Latin).

**B.C.**

**A.D.**

**p.36**
Bronze *hu*
*13th-12th century
B.C.*

**p.40**
Wooden
coffin and
mummy
*about 1000
B.C.*

**p.74**
Black-figured
kylix
*570-565 B.C.*

**p.77**
Red-figured
calyx-krater
*340 B.C.*

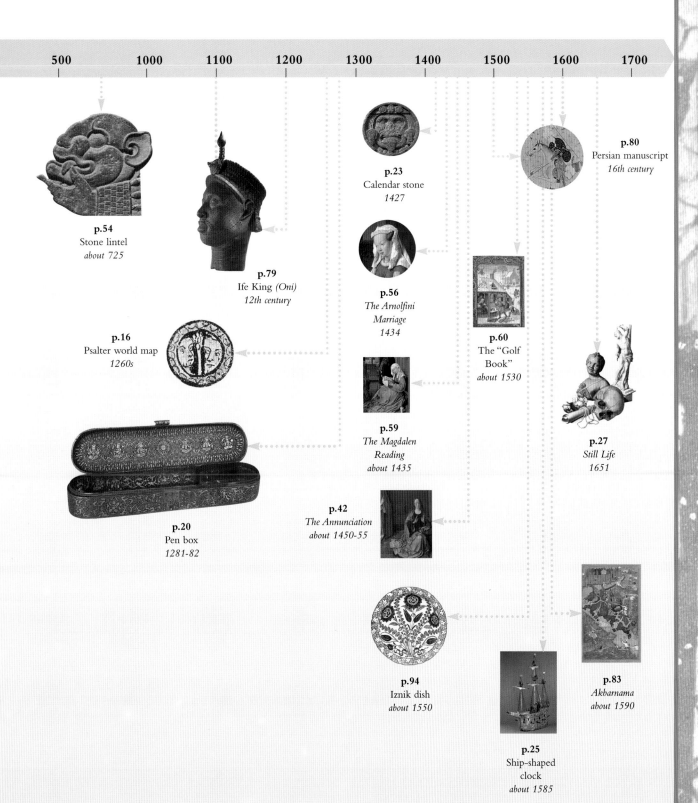

500    1000    1100    1200    1300    1400    1500    1600    1700

**p.54**
Stone lintel
*about 725*

**p.79**
Ife King *(Oni)*
*12th century*

**p.23**
Calendar stone
*1427*

**p.80**
Persian manuscript
*16th century*

**p.16**
Psalter world map
*1260s*

**p.56**
The Arnolfini
Marriage
*1434*

**p.60**
The "Golf
Book"
*about 1530*

**p.59**
The Magdalen
Reading
*about 1435*

**p.27**
*Still Life*
*1651*

**p.20**
Pen box
*1281-82*

**p.42**
*The Annunciation*
*about 1450-55*

**p.94**
Iznik dish
*about 1550*

**p.83**
*Akbarnama*
*about 1590*

**p.25**
Ship-shaped
clock
*about 1585*

1700　　　　1800　　　　1825　　　　1850

**p.45**
Conch-shell
trumpet
*about 1800*

**p.18**
The Crystal Palace
Game
*1854*

**p.62**
*Before the Ball*
*1735*

**p.96**
*Gum-plant and
Kangooroo*
*1789*

**p.64**
Fly whisk
*collected* 1825

**p.99**
*The Great Wave*
*about 1830*

**p.47**
The God A'a
*pre-1821*

**p.101**
Plaque of butterflies
*about 1830*

1875          1900          1950          2000

**p.66**
Centennial album
quilt
*1876*

**p.50**
*Nkondi statue*
*about 1900*

**p.28**
*Galloping*
*1878-79*

**p.102**
*Irises*
*1889*

**p.86**
Sioux winter count
*1900-15*

**p.30**
*Bush Banana*
*Dreaming*
*1980s*

**p.84**
Shadow puppet
*about 1900*

**p.88**
The Magical Breadfruit
Tree
*collected 1948*

**p.49**
Transformation
mask
*collected 1880*

**p.71**
Pende mask
*collected 1910*

**p.105**
*The Water-Lily Pond*
*1899*

# Glossary

**Abstract art** Art that does not show recognizable pictures but instead expresses a feeling or idea with colors or shapes.

**Afterlife** The life of the soul after the body dies.

**Altar** A table or raised place on which sacrifices are offered or religious actions performed.

**Artisan** A skilled craftsperson.

**Basalt** A hard, dark rock from volcanoes.

**Brass** A yellow metal that is a mixture of copper and zinc.

**Brocade** An expensive cloth woven in a raised design.

**Bust** A painting or sculpture showing a person's head and shoulders.

**Byzantine empire** An ancient empire with its capital in Constantinople, now Istanbul in present-day Turkey. Ruled by the Romans from 395 A.D., it then became Christian and eventually collapsed in 1453.

**Calligraphy** Beautiful handwriting, done with pen and ink, for special documents or letters.

**Casting** The process of making objects by pouring hot liquid metal into a mold. The metal hardens and the mold is taken off. This process can be used to make many copies of an object.

**Ceramic** Objects made from clay, often glazed and fired or baked.

**Chieftain** The leader of a clan or tribe.

**Clan** A group of related families who share ancestors and often live in the same area.

**Copper** A red-orange metal. It resists rust and is easily shaped.

**Corrosion** When metal is eaten away and damaged by chemicals in the environment. Rust is a type of corrosion.

**Crest** A decoration on a family or ruler's coat of arms, which can be used to identify them.

**Dynasty** A series of rulers from the same family.

**Emblem** A visual sign that represents an idea, a group, or a person.

**Epic** A long poem about the heroes of a clan or nation.

**Flemish** The people or language of Flanders, a country that no longer exists but used to cover large parts of today's Belgium and Holland.

**Flint** A very hard, gray or brown quartz, often found in chalky earth and used in the Stone Age to make tools.

**Gilding** The process of covering surfaces of objects with a thin layer of gold.

**Gouache** A type of paint, thickened with chalk and gum to make it more opaque or cloudy than watercolor.

**Graffiti** Painting or writing on a public surface, often carried out spontaneously or illegally.

**Horoscope** The prediction of the future by charting where the planets are at certain times, for example when a person is born.

**Initiation** Marking a person's entry into a new social group or a stage in life.

**Inlay** To set into a surface as a decoration or design, for example to set ivory into wood.

**Inscription** Words written as a sign or label, or on a special thing such as a monument, gift, or document.

**Insignia** The sign or badge of a person or group.

**Ivory** A hard, white material from elephant tusks, often carved to make decorative items.

**Jade** A hard, green stone, often used to make decorative items, especially in China.

**Limestone** A type of rock used for buildings and sculpture. Marble is a type of limestone.

**Lintel** A horizontal beam or stone above a window or door.

**Lotus**  A large water lily, a sacred symbol for many peoples, particularly Hindus, Buddhists, and the ancient Egyptians.

**Masquerade**  A party or play at which people wear masks or disguises.

**Medallion**  A medal, or a medal-shaped ornament, often worn around the neck on a chain.

**Mother-of-pearl**  The hard, glossy lining of the pearl oyster. It is often used to make beads and buttons.

**Motif**  The theme or main design of a work of art.

**Myth**  An invented story, usually trying to answer questions about the origins of humankind and nature.

**Oil paint**  A mixture of pigment and oil that makes a long-lasting paint.

**Palette**  A thin board used by an artist to lay out and mix paints.

**Papyrus**  A tall water plant used by the ancient Egyptians, Greeks, and Romans to make a kind of paper.

**Perspective**  The art of painting on a flat surface so that it gives the illusion of distance or depth.

**Pigment**  The part of paint that provides color. It is usually a dry powder taken from rocks, earth, plants, or chemicals.

**Plaque**  A decorative panel or tile hung on or set into walls.

**Raffia**  Fibers from a type of palm tree that can be used for weaving or tying.

**Relief**  A technique in which figures and designs stand out from the surface of a work of art.

**Renaissance**  The period of European history between the 1300s and 1600s, known for its revival of ancient art and learning.

**Ritual**  A series of actions carried out for sacred purposes or at a special event such as a wedding or funeral.

**Sacred**  Something that is holy or special, set apart from everyday life.

**Sacrifice**  To give up something valuable to a god, or to various gods, often as a means to gain protection from them.

**Saga**  A long story of a hero or family.

**Semi-divine**  To appear in human form, but thought to contain an aspect of a god.

**Semiprecious stones**  Stones, like amethyst and garnet, that are not quite as rare and valuable as precious stones like diamonds.

**Shah**  The title given to the rulers of Persia (present-day Iran).

**Silhouette**  An outline of a person or object filled in with one color, usually black.

**Stencil**  A sheet with a design cut out of it. The sheet is laid on a flat surface and paint is applied through the holes.

**Sultan**  A title given to the rulers of certain Muslim countries.

**Symbol**  Something that stands for or represents another object or idea; for example, a heart is a symbol of love.

**Terra-cotta**  Hard, red earthenware, unglazed and often used for pots and tiles.

**Turquoise**  A greenish-blue semiprecious stone.

**Vessel**  A hollow holder such as a cup or pot.

**Vignette**  A small decorative image, usually found in a book.

**Watercolor**  A paint thinned with water instead of oil, which creates a soft and "washy" effect.

**Woodblock print**  A print made from wooden blocks. Often, several blocks each provide colors or lines to complete the final image.

# Index

# Photographic Acknowledgments

For permission to reproduce the illustrations on the following pages and for supplying photographs, the Publishers would like to thank:

© Africa Museum Tervuren, Belgium: 50-51 (photo R. Asselberghs)
AKG London: 26-27
Dr Paul Bahn: 10-11 below and 92-93
The British Library: 12 above left and 60 (Add.24098. f.22v), 14-15 and
16-17 (Add.28681 f.9), 18-19 (Maps 28.667), 61 (Add.24098. f.18v)
© The British Museum: 12 below right and 20-21, 13 above right,
90-91 and 98-99, 13 below right and 40, 24-25, 30-31, 32-33 and
38-39, 34-35, 36-37, 41, 46-47, 70-71, 94-95, 100-101
Photograph © 1998 The Detroit Institute of Arts: 86-87
(gift of Mr & Mrs Richard A. Pohrt)
The J. Paul Getty Museum: 8 and 102-103 (90.PA.20), 12 below left and
62-63, (84.PA.668), 13 above left and 74-75 (85.AE.121),
28-29 (85.XO.362.44), 42-43 (85.PA.24), 76-77 (81.AE.78)
© Milwaukee Public Museum: 88-89
The National Gallery, London: 13 below left and 104-105, 56-57, 58-59
The Natural History Museum, London: 96-97
Shelburne Museum, Vermont: 6, 52-53, 66-67 and 68-69
Arctic Studies Center, National Museum of Natural History,
Smithsonian Institution: 11 above and 48-49
V&A Picture Library: 5, 72-73 and 82-83
Werner Forman Archive: 12 above right and 84-85, 44-45,
54-55, 78-79, 80-81
Courtesy of the Division of Anthropology, Yale Peabody Museum © Peabody
Museum of Natural History, Yale University; New Haven, Connecticut: 64-65


**COVER PICTURES, CLOCKWISE FROM TOP:**
*Galloping* (detail), Edweard Muybridge, England, 1878-79
Calendar Stone (detail), Aztec, 1427
Transformation Mask, Alaska, collected about 1880
*Irises* (detail), Vincent van Gogh, Netherlands, 1889
Puppet, Java, about 1900
Wooden Coffin and Mummy of an Unknown Priestess, Egypt,
21st Dynasty, about 1000 B.C.
Psalter World Map, England, early 1260s (background picture)